Photo © SDP Media. Used with permission.

Penny Mackieson is an Australian social worker and author who was adopted as a newborn and has worked primarily in the children and family services sector. She has Bachelor and Master's degrees in Social Work from the University of Melbourne, where she is currently enrolled in PhD studies to explore permanency in out-of-home care, including the history, purpose and outcomes of Permanent Care Orders. Penny lives with her husband and son in inner Melbourne.

Other books by Penny Mackieson

Real Women Love Footy
(co-authored with Dawn Leicester, 2003)

ADOPTION DECEPTION

A personal and professional journey

PENNY MACKIESON

SPINIFEX

First published by Spinifex Press, 2015

Spinifex Press Pty Ltd
504 Queensberry Street
North Melbourne, Victoria, 3051
Australia
women@spinifexpress.com.au
www.spinifexpress.com.au

Editors: Renate Klein and Pauline Hopkins
Cover design: Deb Snibson
Typesetting: Helen Christie
Typeset in Berthold Baskerville and Museo Sans
Indexer: Karen Gillen
Printed by McPherson's Printing Group
Cover photo courtesy of the author

National Library of Australia Cataloguing-in-Publication data:
Mackieson, Penny, 1963 – author
Adoption deception: a personal and professional journey / Penny Mackieson

9781742199740 (paperback)
9781742199696 (ebook : pdf)
9781742199726 (ebook : epub)
9781742199702 (ebook : Kindle)
Includes bibliographical references and index

Adoption–Australia–History
Adoption–Government policy–Australia
Adoption–Law and legislation–Australia
Australia–Politics and government–1965-
Australia–Social conditions–1965-
362.7340994

MIX
Paper from responsible sources
FSC® C001695
FSC www.fsc.org

For my mothers.

"I am not one and simple, but complex and many."
Virginia Woolf, *The Waves*

CONTENTS

ACKNOWLEDGEMENTS

I owe many thanks in relation to this book. To all the team at Spinifex, especially Renate Klein for letting me to talk her into it; and Pauline Hopkins who, in tandem with Renate, embraced the project with great enthusiasm, insight, expertise and care. To everyone associated with VANISH, especially Coleen Clare and Pauline Ley for being wonderful role models and for their encouragement and support. To my social worker comrades for all the years of professionalism, teamwork, leadership, challenging discussions, honest feedback and generous friendship and support; especially my revered mentors and closest confidantes, Jenny and Cath. To my non-social worker comrades for their inspiration, especially Martin for his own words and mentorship of mine, and David for his music. To my family, especially my partner Bruce, our son Paddy, my mother Carol, and my sister Nicole – for your love, acceptance and loyalty, and for your trust in the sharing of our story.

I am privileged to have so many compassionate, intelligent, egalitarian, ethical, courageous, resilient, nurturing and talented people in my life. My love and gratitude to each and every one of you.

PREFACE

It is a pleasure for me to write the Preface to this book. Penny Mackieson is a member of the Committee of Management of VANISH, the Victorian Adoption Network for Information and Self Help. In my position as Manager of VANISH, I work closely with Penny and I have followed the writing of this book with great anticipation and an understanding of how important its messages are for the whole of the adoption community. *Adoption Deception: A personal and professional journey* conveys the power of one person to unravel the challenging and difficult story of an adopted person; each paragraph resonates with the stories we hear every day from the people we work with at VANISH.

Penny has taken her personal story and analysed it through the lens of her experiences, her profession as a social worker, and her career working in child protection and adoption. She eloquently shares these insights with the reader. As well, she takes us with her on her spirited campaign to expose the simplistic mistakes inherent in the celebrity push for 'one-stop' adoption backed up by popular magazines and television programs which show us images of a happy baby nestled in a happy new family. They disregard the fact that the baby has been torn from a grieving mother, a culture and an extended family.

In the post-adoption work we engage in at VANISH, we regularly face the challenge of helping the community – and especially people who work in child and family welfare – to understand the process of adoption and its lifelong impact. Placing a child deemed to be 'at risk' into an adoptive family is not a simple 'happy ever after' solution to a pressing problem. Penny Mackieson had a loving and supportive adoptive family with whom she remains connected and is a highly qualified and experienced social worker with a long history of working in adoption. Who better to address the complexities of adoption? She generously and intelligently shares her lifelong journey with the reader.

As VANISH lobbies and talks with those in governments who make the legislation, policies and guidelines that so dramatically affect the lives of mothers, fathers and adopted people, we can use this book to help them understand how being separated from one's mother, father, potential family, and extended family, is a traumatic event. Trauma results from the severing of the heartbeat listened to for nine months and the removal of the multitude of senses and systems that have kept the infant connected to her or his own flesh and blood. We know this may have dire consequences for the separated baby and for the mother; the loss is a lifelong tragedy. We know this because over twenty-five years many VANISH service users who search for their mothers, fathers, daughters or sons have told us so. In support groups, we hear how the seemingly happiest adopted children and adolescents nevertheless felt not completely connected, not quite in the right place, intermittently very sad, confused and often lost in a void of wondering and fantasy about who they might have been if they had remained with their parents.

Penny's dedication to helping people understand what adoption means for the mother and the adopted person is palpable and results in a vibrant story that will resonate with many readers. Her stamina and persistence in educating the public about the pain of adoption is seen throughout her story, and in the description of the media campaign that she continually wages. She tries to bring some balance and honesty to the current media bias that suggests a baby can easily be given to another family without sorrow or damage.

Currently in Australia, the pendulum is fast swinging back from a time of rapidly and appropriately diminishing adoption which began in the 1970s to a period that suggests there is a 'right to parent' and that society is obliged to find – or make – babies for infertile couples. The facts tell us that this can mean a lifetime of sadness for mother and child. Surrogacy and intercountry adoption often lead to child stealing and trafficking. Our hearts have been saddened to hear of recent stories from reliable sources of babies abducted from rural Thai mothers and made available for adoption as orphans in Singapore.

Adoption Deception is particularly important at this time when ill-informed policy changes led from the Prime Minister's office and supported by groups such as Adopt Change and Women's Forum Australia are leading to rapid moves to make both domestic and intercountry adoption faster and easier with no evidence-based outcomes to ascertain whether more adoptions are in the best interests of children and the adults they become. Our work at VANISH, listening to the voices of those who have lived through separation from a child and the adoption process, regularly informs us that the loss and grief that follow the adoption experience lasts a lifetime, is often traumatic and entails great sadness and distress. Usually the people we work with don't take the time to write up their experiences into a book. I am grateful to Penny Mackieson that she has done exactly that.

Adoption Deception alerts us to take stock before we return to an era where there is a rush to more adoptions so that infertile families can once again seize other people's babies as their own, thus compounding the mistakes of the past for which the nation has only just apologised.

I am one of those mothers who is blessed with a wonderful son via adoption but I have also witnessed the sorrow and trauma for my son and for his mother that the adoption created and I have seen the never-ending challenges that come from forced separation. The price of adoption is simply too high to pay. Penny knows this from her own experience and she is willing to share her story for the benefit of us all.

It takes courage to put one's life, one's family and one's career on the line in such a detailed and brave manner. Many adopted people will be joyous that someone has told it like it is and will be pleading with the legislators, policy makers and practitioners to take the time to listen to Penny Mackieson's heartfelt messages.

This exposé of what it is really like to be a child – and adult – of adoption is an enormously valuable addition to the ongoing research we need to honestly inform legislation, policies and guidelines. *Adoption Deception: A personal and professional journey* will bring comfort to those who have experienced separation from a child through adoption and will help inform practitioners and the general public.

Coleen Clare
Manager VANISH
Melbourne 2015

INTRODUCTION

This book is grounded in the complexity and interconnectedness of my personal experiences as an adopted person; my professional experiences as a social worker; and my political perspective as a socialist and feminist. The specific catalyst that motivated me to write this book is my outrage about the injustices, human rights violations and exploitation I see in the policies on adoption developed by recent and current neo-liberal governments in Australia. After hearing me talk about these issues, a good friend recently said to me, "Oh, Pen! You're not going to let this adoption thing define who you are, are you?" I replied, "Well, as I was adopted at birth, it's a bit late for that!" However, it is never too late to try and improve a situation – which is what I hope the messages contained in this book will do.

Australia has an unfortunate history of favouring the desires of the most powerful over the rights of the most vulnerable in its legislation, policies and practices concerning the welfare of children. Past mistakes in adoption policies may be forgiven on the basis of an earlier lack of understanding of the long-term consequences. Yet, there is no excuse for quickly forgetting the detrimental consequences of those mistakes, especially as they have been illuminated by formal state, territory and national apologies from 2006 through to 2013. Sadly, however, not only have unethical and/or poor child welfare practices continued, they are in fact becoming even more popular, prevalent and institutionalised in this country.

All parties claim to be acting in the 'best interests of the child' – a variously defined and somewhat rubbery concept with a strong tendency to change over time. Yet, *the perspective of the child* is too often ignored in this debate. In particular, there is a general failure to acknowledge that an adopted person will be an adult for much longer than he or she will be a child subject to the whims of self-interested adults making policies and decisions concerning their 'best interests' that will affect them for the whole of their lives.

Lobby groups in concert with mainstream Australian media have hijacked the debate, saturating public discourse with the perspectives of new and intending parents. They trivialise and play down the negatives and legacies of previous practices and dismiss them as irrelevant. It is as if since 'sorry' has been publicly stated they feel free to repeat and compound the wrongs of past adoption policies and practices with renewed vigour under a legitimised cloak of modernity.

As the new prime minister, Tony Abbott made a personal commitment in December 2013 to streamlining processes and procedures in Australia for the purpose of making it much easier and faster for intending parents to adopt a child from overseas. This is evidence of the resumption of a populist retrograde approach to adoption at the highest level which treats it as a family formation service for middle-class adults, rather than as an alternative family program for vulnerable children. As eminent adoption historians, Professor Emerita Marian Quartly, Professor Shurlee Swain and Professor Denise Cuthbert, have concluded (Quartly, Swain and Cuthbert, 2013, p. 2):

> … a market in children has long existed in Australia, shaped by supply and demand: the demand of those seeking to adopt, and the supply of babies available for adoption.

I am aware that many adoptive parents and people in the general community, as well as some old school child welfare professionals, find the term 'market in children' offensive – too harsh, too confronting. Yet, for many other child welfare professionals and adopted people like me, this bold language is a breath of fresh air, a statement of fact, the language of reality – a reality that this book endeavours to explore.

CHAPTER 1

A brown-eyed baby girl

On 10 March 1963, a healthy baby girl with dark brown eyes and dark brown hair weighing seven pounds seven ounces was born at the Queen Victoria Hospital in Melbourne. She struggled to digest the formula milk the nurses insisted on feeding her. Still, within a few weeks she was deemed ready to leave.

On 1 April 1963, the baby arrived at her new home – a modest timber cottage in the small rural township of Buchan South in East Gippsland, in eastern Victoria. The parents seated their other child – an almost three-year-old boy with blue eyes and white-blonde hair – on the green vinyl couch in their lounge room facing the fireplace. The baby – swaddled tightly in a bunny rug – was carefully placed on the boy's lap. He instinctively wrapped his arms around her and gazed searchingly into her face. She returned his gaze with the unblinking intensity characteristic of newborns. Lulled by the rhythmic motion and noise of the long car journey, the baby had just woken from a deep sleep and this was not what she had expected. For several minutes neither child moved, each content to explore the other's face. Eventually, the baby felt a warm sensation invade her body.

"Mummy," the little boy said calmly and without breaking eye contact with his new sister. "Bubby's wet herself."

That brown-eyed baby girl was, in fact, me. I was adopted, as were the brother with whom I was raised and five of our cousins. And this was my first encounter with my new brother in my new family.

I recall my childhood as mostly happy; my experiences growing up as generally positive. I always knew that I was adopted, so it was never a secret or a shock to me. My adoptive parents – who I will always fondly call 'Mum' and 'Dad' – openly told my brother and me about our adoptions from the time of our respective arrivals in the family. Not that they really had a choice, living as we did in a small close-knit rural community in which Mum operated the local post office and manual telephone exchange: a 24/7 service. It would have been impossible to explain to her many daily customers how two babies, the first aged one week and the second a few years later aged three weeks, had arrived when she had not shown any signs of pregnancy.

I have always felt that my brother and I were deeply loved and adored by Mum and Dad. There is no doubt that they made many personal sacrifices to ensure we had everything we needed, and got as much of what we wanted as they could reasonably afford. They were not wealthy or educated people, though intelligent and well-read. They always managed what income and assets they had very well.

However, as I remember it, from a young age my life has included complexities that influenced my behaviour as a child; legacies that have also been at the forefront of my responses and decision-making throughout my adulthood. For example, when I started dating and seeking a life partner it was very important to me that the young man – and thus I – knew his parentage. The thought of accidentally partnering with someone who might have been closely related biologically frightened me.[1] In fact, in 1980 – the year I commenced tertiary studies, the ratio of adopted people to non-adopted people in Australia would have been such that many unknowingly biologically related adoptees would likely have partnered and produced offspring. I recently calculated this ratio to be approximately 1:58, based on an estimated 250,000 (legal/registered) adoptions having occurred in Australia from the late 1920s to the early 1980s,[2] and the population of Australia having been approximately 14,500,000 in 1980.[3] I find this deeply worrying and unacceptable. Yet, I am even more alarmed that I have never heard of any particular concerns held or raised about it by any Australian commentators – welfare professionals, academics, social policy analysts, politicians or general community members alike.

My budding social work skills got plenty of practice during my first casual explorations of the family backgrounds of boyfriends. When I got married at the age of almost 26, I could not embrace changing my family name to my husband's – not that I found anything distasteful or wrong with his name; quite the contrary, as I had always considered it an Irish variation of my adoptive Scottish one. Some people may believe that I refused to change my family name because I am a feminist. But at that time, my feminist perspective was not particularly strong. It was also still very important for me to make decisions of which my adoptive parents approved. However, on this occasion, Mum and Dad's approval was less important than

1 Later I learned that my innate caution was vindicated due to the phenomenon of 'genetic sexual attraction' that often occurs between people who meet years after separation through adoption. It is the result of identifying with someone who physically resembles one's self for, perhaps, the first time in one's life and the intense feelings, hopes and expectations aroused on finally being reunited with them (see Fitsell, 1994).

2 See Inglis (1984), as quoted by Higgins (2010), p. 7.

3 Source: Australian Bureau of Statistics <http://www.abs.gov.au/ausstats/abs@.nsf/Lookup/by%20Subject/1301.0~2012~Main%20Features~Population%20size%20and%20growth~47//>.

not having another identity change forced upon me simply because I had a new legal status.

Another example of how my adoption has always influenced my decision-making and behaviour is that, from as far back as I can remember, I tried hard to fit in to my adoptive family and thus not risk rejection, or as I perceived it, another 'abandonment'. I always had a nagging feeling that my adoptive brother was, quite literally, 'the golden-haired boy'. He was the first child in the family; the child my adoptive parents had longed for. Yes, he was a handful – probably hyperactive; probably the behavioural manifestation of his own insecurities and a legacy from his separation at birth from his own mother. But he was emotionally engaging and had a way about him that other people responded to warmly, and so he was quickly forgiven for any misdemeanours. Mum told me several times that the Anglican minister who had assisted her and Dad to adopt my brother was visiting them one day when he suggested it was about time they adopted a sister for their son. This has never felt like a very auspicious entrée into my adoptive family.

I sensed from very early on that learning and education were very important to my adoptive parents. I became verbal at a young age and had learned to read and write by the time I commenced schooling in Grade Prep – there was no kindergarten available in the area during the early years of my childhood. After just three weeks of Prep schooling, I was 'put up' (promoted) to Grade 1, as my primary teachers and adoptive parents considered I was not sufficiently challenged academically by the Prep curriculum. I thus became and remained 12–18 months younger than the majority of my same grade peers throughout my education – turning eight in Year 4, 13 in Year 9, and so on. When I was in Grade 5, my adoptive brother was in Grade 6, but we shared the same maths class. It was clear to me, even then, that this undermined his academic confidence. Meanwhile, I had already internalised significant family expectation and pressure to continue maintaining a top three academic position in every subject so that I would continue to receive the approval of my adoptive parents. Ultimately, I even managed to achieve third place at my secondary school in Year 12 (Higher School Certificate) in 1979, with a special distinction in one subject – biology.

Apparently, I presented as mature for my grade as well as for my years. This was demonstrated by an incident on the school bus when I was 12 and in Year 8. The bus driver chastised me for not having demonstrated better leadership with a group of other junior secondary students who were making a lot of noise and distracting him – he later admitted he had thought I was 15. I was 19 when I was first asked to provide proof of age at a pub, but I still had to apply for an age exemption in order to enrol in first year tertiary studies before turning 17, and then another in order to transfer into social work studies before turning 19.

Buchan South Primary School was a very small school, located right next door to my adoptive family home. Only 35 children were enrolled there at its peak during the years of my primary schooling (1968–1973), and enrolment numbers steadily declined after that. The school was closed down altogether in the early 1980s when enrolments dropped to fewer than seven. There had been seven children in my grade – it was one of the largest grades at the school at the time. The students were all from farming and labouring families in the local district. Generally speaking, they were not a particularly academic lot and so I stood out – for the right reasons as far as my adoptive parents were concerned, but for the wrong reasons for the local community. I was awarded Dux in my first year and have always treasured the illustrated storybook, *The Wolf and the Kids*, I received as the prize, inscribed with the words, 'Presented to Penny Mackieson, Dux of Infant Department, Buchan South No. 3256, 1968.' But the other parents objected and the award of Dux was discontinued from the following year onwards, replaced with awards such as 'Best Attendance' and 'Most Improved Student', so that the other children would be assured of also receiving the accolades.

Resentment regarding my relative academic prowess culminated when I was in Grade 6. When not attending school, my brother and I typically spent much time outdoors playing as well as assisting Dad and Mum on our small family farm. I am pale-skinned, like many people of Celtic-Anglo origin, but my skin was tanned in those days, though with a yellowish rather than brown, tone. My brown eyes were somewhat almond-shaped, and I often wore my thick dark brown hair in a bob-style cut. My appearance, combined with my scholastic abilities, triggered a brief period of bullying during which some students teased me at school by calling me 'Ching-Chong'. Apparently, they – or, perhaps, their parents – believed that only Asian children could be as 'clever' as I was. Because everyone knew I was adopted and my genetic background was therefore unknown, the implication was that I must have been of Asian origin. There were no Asian people in our small community – indeed, in our entire district – and, ludicrously, it was considered a horrible insult at that time to be compared with Asians. Actually, there were very few people in the district of non-Celtic-Anglo heritage, including very few Indigenous Australians. The children were careful not to mention my adoptive status when they teased me. But I felt the derogatory term 'bastard' was never far from their lips. This was probably as instructed by their parents, given the respect and esteem in which my adoptive parents were held in regard to their significant contributions to the local community. But it hurt my feelings deeply. I was ten at the time and considered my new tormentors to be my oldest friends.

The following year, my grade peers and I parted ways as we progressed to the nearest High and Technical schools in Bairnsdale, a 45-mile bus ride away. I attended Bairnsdale High School and was placed in an all-girls class of 35 – the same size as my entire primary school had been. There were well over 1,000 students enrolled at Bairnsdale High School at the time, about 240 of them in Year 7, and there was no one else from my Grade 6 in my Year 7 class. The scale of things had upsized dramatically, and so I felt even more pressure to maintain my high standard of academic achievement.

By then my adoptive brother had been well and truly ensconced as the sporting child of the family – even though I was also quite good at sports and equally enjoyed playing them. I tacitly understood that my role was prescribed as the academic child.

There were other politics at play within my adoptive family. Even though Mum and Dad were open in sharing with us what little they claimed they knew of our background stories, I was acutely aware that my brother and I were expected to act as if our lives had started when we were placed in the Mackieson household. There was a powerful, though unspoken, expectation that we should accept this without question – to the extent that over the years I was forced to be honest, overt and repetitious in expressing to Mum my position on two particular matters. Firstly, while I was interested in her passionate hobby of researching the genealogy of her own and Dad's families (as well as the local district history), I did not wish to become the custodian of Mum's extensive history collections after she was gone. I could never bring myself to state it to her this boldly, but I did not feel a genuine sense of connection to my adoptive parents' family histories. I privately resented Mum's apparent insensitivity and relentlessness in pushing me to be more involved in, and responsible for, maintaining these links. Secondly, I did not yet know if or when I might ever wish to search for information regarding, or make contact with, members of my own family of origin, though I had no inclination to do so while I was growing up or attending university.

A further example of the complexities and legacies of my

life is that I was never told that my mother had named me on registering my birth. Mum and Dad must have known at least my first name as given to me by my mother from my legal adoption paperwork, but they never revealed it to me. So I always had the impression that my original name was chosen by Mum and Dad. Indeed, they often told me how Dad had chosen my first name, 'Penelope', because he especially liked it, and how Mum had chosen my second name, 'Kathleen', after her own mother's first name. As a child and teenager I always assumed that my birth must have been registered referring to me simply as 'Baby X' or something similar.

In 1990 – by which time I was in my late 20s, a qualified social worker with a Master's degree, married, and contemplating having children of my own – I applied to the then Department of Community Services Victoria (CSV) to seek any relevant medical information pertaining to my mother from my adoption records.

It was only then that I discovered my mother had given me both a first and a second name, as well as her family name. I also discovered that the narrative I had always believed to be true regarding my mother's circumstances was not correct. My adoptive parents had consistently told me that my mother resided in an inner northern Melbourne suburb – perhaps Brunswick – and that she was a secondary school student who wished to continue her education and progress to university. This seemed plausible enough, given my own academic inclinations. Also, as I went through my undergraduate social work placements and subsequently worked in the profession, clients in the western suburbs of Melbourne from Italian, Greek, Croatian – in fact, from whatever European ethnic background they came – often started speaking to me in their native language and simply assumed I shared the same cultural heritage as they did.

But in 1990 I learnt that my mother was of Anglo heritage; resided in the Latrobe Valley; and had already left secondary school by the time she conceived me. I was shocked to the core and felt unable to share my discovery with my adoptive mother (my adoptive father had already died, in late 1988, just three months prior to my wedding). In response, I carefully stored away the near illegible photocopies provided to me of my original adoption documents. I felt overwhelmed and unable to deal with this new information.

What shocked me more than anything, though, is that my mother had given me two perfectly lovely names – 'Lisa Jane'; names of the same genre as those with which Mum and Dad had re-named me. Most hurtful was that 'Lisa' was the first name given to the firstborn child of my adoptive family's neighbours – a girl about 18 months younger than me who had been my best friend until her family moved away during my primary schooling. I was struck by an overwhelming feeling of injustice – that my friend should not have been given that name; that another name would have needed to be chosen for her *if I had been allowed to keep my name.*

For the first time in my life it really hit home that I had been re-labelled, re-badged and recycled into a format acceptable to my adoptive parents; that my origins had been deliberately wiped away; that the feelings I had experienced since early childhood in relation to needing to fit in with my adoptive family were, after all, based on real rather than imagined expectations; that receiving the love and acceptance of my adoptive parents was conditional upon me playing *by their rules.*

These were – and continue to be – complex feelings, difficult to digest and not easily resolved, not least because I have always dearly loved and deeply respected my adoptive parents and have never wished to deliberately upset them or hurt their feelings. I have always empathised with the emotional pain they themselves experienced through their infertility and inability to produce the biological offspring they so deeply desired. Family relationships, family history and family connections were very important to my adoptive parents, especially to Mum.

I consider myself to be an innately loyal person, yet I have found my loyalties uncomfortably divided. I am very grateful for the love and care and opportunities provided to me by my adoptive parents, yet I can never be grateful for having been forcibly separated from my mother at birth; for having had my name, my identity, changed; for having grown up feeling like I never quite fitted in, no matter how hard I tried; for having subsequently struggled all my life with identity and self-esteem issues; for having missed out on growing up with my mother and biological siblings. Similarly, no matter how many times I was told by well-meaning adoptive relatives, family friends and acquaintances while growing up that I was 'lucky' to have been adopted by Mum and Dad, I always felt ambivalent about being instructed that this was how I should feel.

As alluded to earlier, I returned to Melbourne in 1980 to undertake social work studies. I completed Bachelor and Master Degrees in Social Work at Melbourne University in 1983 and 1989, and subsequently worked primarily in Victoria's children and family services sector, including within the child protection program. I was drawn to helping vulnerable people, hence my choice of career as a social worker. I soon learned that this was a common calling for adopted people. During my third year of tertiary studies, a social work lecturer asked those in the class who were adopted to raise their hands. I knew for a fact that one other young woman in the class was also adopted but got a real jolt when, including the two of us, about a third of the 25 or so students present raised their hands. Interestingly, when I attended the Tenth Australian Adoption Conference in Melbourne in 2012, I found that social work also seemed to be a common profession for mothers who 'relinquished' their babies during the era of my adoption. I have observed that social work and related professions are occupations not infrequently chosen by intercountry adoptees, though the latter seem to be an artistic cohort, too.

I have to admit that I was not, however, drawn to working in the field of adoption. As a young adult I felt it might pose a significant conflict of interest – something politicians, in particular, seem not to appreciate at all these days. But I had never forbidden myself from working in adoption, just as I never forbade myself from seeking information about or contact with my family of origin. Consistent with knowledge acquired in my social work training and practice, I found that my responses to various events in my life caused me to change my perspective on this matter over time.

The first of these events was experiencing my own fertility problems – I was diagnosed with blocked fallopian tubes at the age of 30 in 1993. Our specialist informed my husband and me that we were ideal candidates for in vitro fertilisation (IVF). After much research and discussion, we decided to undergo IVF treatment – but only with *our own ova and sperm.* It was very important to me that, should the circumstances arise, we would never use any donor ova or donor sperm – as this would necessitate other people relinquishing their potential children. Having been adopted, I could not embrace the concept of being an adoptee with ongoing identity and self-esteem struggles but knowingly creating a child who would more than likely experience the same sorts of lifelong challenges. Similarly, I was adamant that we would not 'donate' any 'leftover' embryos, should we be lucky enough to have a child or children through IVF. Again, I considered this akin to *relinquishing our own potential children* – potential children we had *deliberately created from our own reproductive cells.* I felt committed to giving each embryo we had created the opportunity to implant in my uterus and thus to become a much loved and valued member of *our family.*

I conceived nine months after commencing IVF treatment, as a result of the fourth embryo transfer involving the last (eighth and ninth) embryos created from the first ova collection cycle. (The practice then was that embryos were transferred two at a time, but one embryo did not survive the thawing process prior to transfer.) Looking back, this was relatively quick. Yet, at the time, it felt like slow motion; I even had a month's break from IVF treatment while I travelled overseas with my adoptive mother. Thus in mid-1995, after a difficult full-term labour, our first son was born. Our indescribable joy on becoming parents was tempered by the knowledge that my fertility was declining during my 30s, and so we decided to resume IVF treatment when our son was 12 months of age in order to have a second child.

Again I conceived from the last pair of embryos transferred from the first ova collection cycle of the treatment program. This time it was double the joy! Yet, our elation was all too quickly replaced with a terrible heartache. Early in 1997, 22 weeks and four days into my twin pregnancy, I experienced premature labour. My babies had to be delivered the following day due to a life-threatening risk to me from infection. They passed away within a couple of hours.

I was aware that new grief could revive grief from a previous loss. Indeed, I was also aware that some losses are so painful they might never be fully resolved and are thus always ready to be tapped into with the next loss experience. I had been separated from my mother at birth; my adoptive paternal grandmother died before I was two; one of my closest, and favourite, adoptive cousins died on my eighth birthday; my adoptive maternal grandfather died when I was 12; my adoptive maternal grandmother died when I was 25, three weeks after my engagement; only three weeks after that, my adoptive father died unexpectedly. I experienced intense grief, including some symptoms of depression, after Dad's death, to the extent that I wanted to delay our wedding date. However, both Mum and my fiancé (now husband) insisted on following through with our existing bookings. Mum reiterated several times that it was what Dad would have wanted. As the dutiful daughter I repressed my feelings, my insecurities, and complied. But I struggled to embrace and enjoy the process I knew was normally associated with the lead up to one's wedding. And on the day, holding on to my adoptive brother's arm, I cried all the way down the aisle and was forced to discreetly pat away my tears with my brother's handkerchief (thank goodness it was a clean one!) under the cover of my veil throughout the ceremony. Close inspection of our wedding photos at the church bears witness to my unanticipated outpouring of emotion. I had been ambushed and overwhelmed by the sudden realisation that Dad should have been the one walking me down the aisle; that he should have been present to share my big day. I recovered from that, apart from since then dreading big family celebrations and not being able to fully relax and enjoy family events, especially Christmas and family birthdays.

But then, at the age of 33, I also lost my precious twins – my daughter and my second son. I had not anticipated this – children were not meant to die before their parents. I was more than devastated; I was annihilated. I felt truly alone, emotionally adrift, psychologically lost and abandoned. It was as if the threads of my life – of my very self – were fraying, unravelling, and rapidly so. I slid into an abyss of despair. I wanted to curl up and simply fade from the world; stop drinking, stop eating, stop breathing, willing my heart to stop beating. Yet, at the same time, I knew I could never abandon my precious firstborn son – he needed me more than it was fair to give in to my all-consuming grief. It was not his fault that his siblings had died.

During the following 12 months my resilience flatlined and I experienced periods of depression. Nevertheless, I was determined to weave the threads of my life back together into some sort of whole and secure entity; to rebuild my self-confidence, my identity, myself. I subsequently engaged in a two-year period of individual counselling, followed by a briefer period of marital counselling. It worked and I survived, but I still have to convince myself that I should wear anything other than black clothing for mourning. And we – my husband and I – survived together, in spite of our relationship suffering enormously in the aftermath of our babies' deaths. We even managed to resume IVF treatment for periods at a time, but with no success. We agreed to cease IVF treatment altogether just prior to our son commencing Grade Prep, which was also just prior to my thirty-eighth birthday in 2001. I had no wish to become one of the grey-haired grandmother-aged women desperately persisting with IVF treatment – not knowing how or when to stop trying to have a baby long past the age during which it is feasible for a fertile woman to do so – such as those I had encountered from the very first time I entered an IVF clinic waiting room. Besides, we already had one child whose existence we have both always considered a miracle for which we are extremely fortunate. It was a timely decision as we had no 'leftover' embryos to have to worry about.

Underlying my experience of that first year after my twins died was a need – indeed, a compulsion – to search for my mother and family of origin. I felt strongly that in order to rebuild my identity it needed to be done from the roots up. And so I retrieved from the back of the bottom filing cabinet drawer in our study the large envelope into which I had carefully placed, several years prior, the pages which comprised the copy of my meagre adoption file. With the assistance and support of VANISH, the Victorian Adoption Network for Information and Self Help, I quickly met with success in making contact with my mother, Carol, in 1997. I had prepared myself for the worst-case scenario, so I was rapt and relieved in equal parts that Carol welcomed my first, very carefully worded, letter. We corresponded tentatively for several months exchanging information and photographs via letter before she was ready to tell her two youngest children, who were still living at home, about me. However, she had already told her husband, Pat (not my father), before they were married. I have since been fortunate to have established positive relationships with these members of my family – including a lovely friendship with my sister, Nicole.

Coincidentally, Pat's first name is the same as the name my husband and I gave our first son. Pat's family name, McLernon, is of Scottish origin, as is my adoptive family name, Mackieson. Also, Carol's second child shares the same first name as my adopted brother.[4] And a few years before I had sought information from CSV from my adoption file, my husband and I chose to move to the eastern Melbourne suburb of Kew – the same suburb, as it turned out, of the former site of the Mothers and Babies Home operated by the then Mission of St James and St John (now Anglicare) in which Carol stayed during her pregnancy with me. A further coincidence is that the hospital in which I was born, the Mothers and Babies Home where I grew in my mother's womb and the primary school at which I was educated – each no longer exists.

My experience in seeking contact with my father and his family was not so positive. My father died in 2002, a few months after he phoned me for the first and, as it transpired, only time. The letters and photos I had sent him were subsequently returned to me via post without any letter, note or sender's address – presumably by my father's sister who apparently decided that she wanted nothing to do with me after his death. This was – and still is – a significant disappointment to me. Apparently, I physically resemble my father's side of my family more closely than Carol's. Unfortunately, I never got to meet my father in person; nor have I ever seen a photograph of him or any of his relatives. Carol has said that I look very much like my paternal aunt – the woman who does not wish to know me. Still, I have empathy for my aunt. Carol did not inform my father of her pregnancy with me when she was 16 (in fact, she did not tell anyone) and thus, his details were not recorded on my birth registration. My father only discovered my existence

4 Carol has had six children: first me; then three sons; then second daughter, Nicole; and youngest son, Scott.

when he and Carol happened to cross paths some months after I met her in 1998, by which time I was already 35. Thus I feel that I am not 'real' to my aunt; she never knew about me, never met me as a baby or child, and clearly does not feel a need to meet me as an adult. People react to revelations later in life in a variety of ways; sadly, denial and rejection are some of them.

My experience in sharing with Mum my contact with my family of origin was also not so positive. During the urgency of my efforts to rebuild myself in the aftermath of my twin babies' deaths, I had naively prepared myself better for the possibility of rejection by my maternal family than for the possibility of my adoptive mother not wanting to share this new/old part of my life with me. I told Mum in person when I had established letter contact with Carol, and explained that we were progressing towards a meeting. Mum seemed to take the news quite well at first, noting that she had often wondered over the years *when* I would search for my birth family, as if she had anticipated I would definitely do so at some point in my life. She reiterated the background story she had always shared with me about the circumstances of my birth and relinquishment, despite the fact that the information I shared with her from my adoption file and from Carol's letters differed substantially. To my dismay, within hours of that initial conversation, Mum became very distressed and expressed to me her fear that she would 'lose' me to my birth family. She stated emphatically that she did not wish me to discuss the matter with her ever again. I understood this as a codified instruction: Mum did not want me to take my growing relationship with Carol any further. In fact, she wanted me to cease contact with Carol altogether.

I appreciate that there must have been a lot going on for Mum. She may well have found herself unexpectedly overcome by emotions and feelings similar to those she had experienced when challenged by her infertility as a young woman. My conversation regarding my search and reunion had likely triggered her reliving that difficult experience.

Also, there was no one really close to her still alive that she felt she could share her feelings with, apart from me – but I was also the source of her turmoil. Further, I sensed an equally old and dormant 'judgmentalism' in the way Mum wanted nothing to do with the woman to whom I was born outside the institution of marriage. The hypocrisy inherent in this meant Mum could never verbalise it to me, given her pride in her two adopted children and having embraced my adopted brother's daughter, born in a de facto marital relationship, and his step-daughters as her granddaughters.

Nevertheless I was confused that Mum, always seemingly open about my background previously, was closed to the same subject now. I was also acutely offended that she could possibly think our relationship might change as a result of my contact with my family of origin; that I would love her any less or would want our relationship to be any less close than it had always been. Mum's unwillingness and inability to embrace my reunion with Carol and her family was – at least up to that time – the most hurtful aspect of my adoption journey. It reinforced my long held internalisation – my deepest fear – that my relationship with my Mum had to be on her terms or I would be considered disloyal and not a good daughter; that I would be rejected. I felt like Mum's love was conditional on denial of my own family history, of my own family relationships, of my own true identity … whatever that was. It felt unfair that Mum expected me to end contact with my mother when it had only just begun; this was supposed to be the beginning of a new phase of my life.

I was deeply saddened that I was not free to discuss my maternal family members with Mum, particularly as I knew she had some interests in common with Carol – like gardening and reading romance novels. I was also frustrated that I was not free to discuss my maternal family members with any of my extended adoptive family members – in case they accidentally (or intentionally) mentioned it to Mum and she subsequently became further distressed and upset. Before she died in 2011, Mum asked about my relationship with Carol only once, some ten years after our initial conversation about her. I was honest in my response and Mum quickly changed the subject. I never raised the matter with her again – just as she had originally requested.

Even in this one example of what most people would consider a positive outcome, adoption has had profound and lifelong impacts, not only on the woman who gave up her child and on the adopted person, but also on members of the adoptive family.

I have shared my adoption story for a reason, but not because I think it is particularly interesting. Indeed, over the years I have read many testimonials by other adoptees which could easily have been written by me. Likewise, I have read many testimonials by other mothers who, when young and single, were forced to part with their babies for adoption which could easily have been written by Carol. For example, several such stories are quoted in the pivotal book about the history of adoption in Australia by Quartly, Swain and Cuthbert, *The Market in Babies* (2013).

The primary reason I have shared my personal story is the hope that it will facilitate the reader's understanding of how my perspective on the highly complex, sensitive and emotionally fraught topics of adoption, donor conception and surrogacy has developed. However, before sharing a later stage of my life as a social worker in intercountry adoption, in the following pages is a brief summary of adoption in Australia as it developed from the mid-nineteenth century up to the present day.

CHAPTER 2

A chronology of adoption in Australia

Summarised below are key social and legislative developments regarding adoption in Australia, with a particular focus on the State of Victoria:[5]

1800s: An informal type of fostering/boarding out of children (or 'baby farming': the provision of private board and lodging for babies/infants at commercial rates) was common practice from the mid-1800s. The abuse of baby farming for financial gain and infanticide were not uncommon practices. For example, in her book, *The Baby Farmers* (2013), Annie Cossins pieces together the tragic real-life story of Sarah and John Makin, two destitute baby farmers in inner Sydney, who were found guilty of murdering a baby and were most likely involved in the serial murder or manslaughter of several other babies. This case

> exposed a shocking underworld of desperate mothers, drugged and starving babies, and a black market in the sale and murder

5 Sources include: Adoption and Permanent Care Fact Sheets produced by the Victorian Department of Human Services; the State Library of Victoria website; the VANISH website; Higgins (2011); a Fact Sheet produced by the Centre for Excellence in Child and Family Welfare Inc.; Quartly, Swain and Cuthbert (2013); and the *Commonwealth Contribution to Former Forced Adoption Policies and Practices* (February 2012) report.

of children ... It's a glimpse into a society that preferred to turn a blind eye to the fate of its most vulnerable members, only a century ago (Cossins, 2014).

1840s: In the 1840s, metropolitan newspapers began publishing classified advertisements from both people seeking to adopt children and parents unable to care for their children. The advertisements were for private arrangements that were not authorised by law, and so 'sellers' often advertised a cash payment to cover the costs of the adopting family. There were always more advertisements for children available than from families seeking them. Adoption was not established or regulated as a legal practice and no official adoption records were kept.

1890s: Formal adoption of children was being advocated in Australia from the 1890s by child welfare officials who argued that it would reduce the number of children needing to be maintained in state care. The colonial parliaments were slow to respond: there were no British precedents for such legislation and serious objections were raised in regard to depriving (natural) mothers of their children.

1896: The first Australian legislation to make provision for the adoption of children was introduced in Western Australia in 1896. It required the court to be satisfied that adoption would promote the welfare and interest of the child; that the child was aged under 15 years and, if aged over 12 years, consented to the adoption; that relevant parental or guardian consents had been obtained, unless the child had been deserted; and that the married couple or person adopting the child were of good repute, fit and proper, and had sufficient ability to raise and educate the child. This legislation also terminated all rights and relationships between the child and their (natural) parents and conferred all legal rights and responsibilities for the child on the adopting parents, as if the child had been born to them in lawful wedlock.

1920: Australians became aware that other countries, including America and England, had legislated for adoption. In newspapers, articles reprinted from overseas presented adoption as a wholly benevolent act, despite the erasure of the child's family of origin; stories were sympathetic to Hollywood stars who chose to form their families via adoption; and these happy themes were reinforced in popular films and novels. It was in this context that adoption legislation was introduced in Tasmania in 1920, and in which the other states quickly followed suit.

1923: Adoption legislation was introduced in New South Wales (NSW).

1925: Adoption legislation was introduced in South Australia.

1928: The *Adoption Act* was proclaimed in Victoria, and came into effect in 1929.

> From this time all adoptions had to be registered, giving the adopted child a new legal identity as a member of her adopted family. The exchange of money was made illegal. The introduction of legal adoption dampened but did not eliminate the trade in children (Quartly et al., 2013, p. 2).

1930s: The acts pertaining to adoption were intended to encourage adoptions by providing the new parents security of possession and preventing contact from the child's birth family. However, only a few hundred children were adopted per year in each state under this legislation. Secrecy continued to surround the process of adoption through to the 1960s due to the stigma attached to illegitimacy.

1935: Adoption legislation was introduced in the Northern Territory and Queensland.

1938: Adoption legislation was introduced in the Australian Capital Territory.

1940s: From the 1940s, adoption advocates considered it desirable for relinquishment of the child to happen as soon as possible, preferably immediately after birth, in order to provide a 'clean break'.

1942: The ratio of buyers to sellers advertising in metropolitan newspapers across Australia changed dramatically during the Second World War, with more intending parents seeking children than there were children available and also wanting increased security of possession. State parliaments responded by passing laws which formalised adoptions as closed arrangements, including sealing the child's original birth records and severing all contact with their birth family.

1946: The *Immigration (Guardianship of Children) Act* was introduced by the Commonwealth Government, providing for the federal Minister for Immigration to be the guardian of non-citizen children entering the country for the purposes of adoption, then delegating this responsibility to the secretary of the welfare department of the child's state/territory of residence, ceasing upon grant of a local adoption order or when recognised under the respective state/territory adoption legislation.

1950s–1960s: There were more infants available for adoption than couples wanting to adopt during the 1950s and 1960s. The lack of financial support available and the negative social attitudes prevailing toward single mothers meant women had little choice but to relinquish a child born outside marriage.

The community viewed adoption as a neat way for infertile couples to achieve a family, and for the problem of illegitimacy to be dealt with at the same time. Social workers were authorised to decide which couples were suitable to adopt and which children would be passed as 'fit for adoption'; the implication being that the adoptive parents had a 'right' to a 'perfect' child. Children over the age of six months were considered difficult to place, and children who were older and/or had a disability were generally regarded as unplaceable. Children were physically matched as closely as possible with the adoptive parents in order to pass as substitute biological children of the adoptive parents. These developments were driven by the demands of adopting parents, and single mothers were placed under considerable pressure to relinquish their children.

1966: The *Adoption of Children Act 1964* came into operation in Victoria in January 1966, in the context of 'uniform' adoption legislation enacted in all Australian states and territories during the 1960s. This Act elevated the welfare of the child to being paramount in adoption legislation; and provided for adoptions to be arranged by registered and authorised adoption agencies only, rather than through professionals (such as doctors, lawyers or ministers of religion) or private individuals. This was in response to concerns about the buying and selling of children and unauthorised placements.

1969–1970: The Victorian Council for the Single Mother and Her Child (CSMC) was established using a self-help model with the aims of challenging the stigma of single parenthood; and advocating for and supporting single mothers and their children.

1972: Adoption numbers peaked in 1971–72, with almost 10,000 children adopted across Australia. Following this, the numbers of infants placed for adoption decreased dramatically as a result of several interrelated factors: primarily, increasingly tolerant community attitudes toward ex-nuptial births and single parenthood (the status of 'illegitimacy' disappeared, replaced by the term 'ex-nuptial'); the introduction of government benefits for single parents (by the Labor Whitlam government in 1973); improved contraception; and widespread access to safe pregnancy terminations (abortions). Secondarily, more women joined the workforce; and childcare became increasingly accessible and affordable.

1976: Beginning with NSW in 1976, registers were established in different states for people wishing to make contact with their parents or children separated via adoption.

1980s: Mothers who had relinquished their babies and adults who were adopted as children publicly challenged the practice of adoption, and social workers began assisting young single mothers to keep and care for their babies.

1984: The adoption legislation in Victoria was amended (effective 1985) following a comprehensive review of adoption legislation in the state. The Victorian *Adoption Act 1984* introduced a range of progressive provisions, including the rights for adopted persons (aged 18 or over) to access their original birth certificate and information about their birth parents; for adoption of children only after the provision of informed consent by both birth parents; and for ongoing contact between birth parents and their children following adoption. This legislation marked the introduction of 'open' adoptions in Australia, with similar legislative changes following in the other states.

1985: The Victorian Adoption Information Service (AIS), now known as Family Information Networks and Discovery (FIND), was established in the Department of Community Services (CSV[6]) following proclamation of the *Adoption Act 1984*. The purpose of the service was, and continues to be, to assist people who have been separated by adoption to obtain information about each other from the respective adoption records, and/or to contact each other.

1987: A review conducted by CSV concluded that the AIS needed streamlining. It also recognised that an independent search and support service would help facilitate an efficient adoption information service, and thereby reduce the long waiting list maintained by the AIS.

1989: The Victorian Adoption Network for Information and Self Help (V.A.N.I.S.H.) was established using a self-help model. VANISH was, and has continuously been, funded by the Victorian government through DHHS to provide a specialised search service for adopted persons, and to provide a support service to those affected by adoption. A key difference between the services provided by VANISH and those provided by FIND is that VANISH is not authorised to provide access to applicants to their adoption records. But once a person has obtained their adoption records from FIND, they often prefer to seek the support and guidance of VANISH, a non-government agency, with integrating information and deciding whether to search for their birth parents or family.

1989: The *Convention on the Rights of the Child* was adopted by the United Nations (UN) General Assembly in 1989, entering force in September 1990 and becoming the most widely and rapidly accepted human rights treaty in history.

6 Community Services Victoria (CSV) subsequently became the Department of Human Services (DHS), which under the Andrews Labor government elected in November 2014 merged with the former Department of Health to become the Department of Health and Human Services (DHHS).

December 1990: Australia ratified the *UN Convention on the Rights of the Child (1989).*

1992: Permanent Care Orders were introduced in Victoria, as provided for through the *Children and Young Persons Act 1989.* The concept of permanent care, rather than adoption,

> grew out of the reform movements of the 1970s and 1980s which opened adoption to contact between the birth parent, the child and the adoptive parents and challenged decision making processes and 'welfare drift' within the child welfare system (DHS, *Adoption and Permanent Care Learning Guide, Part 3*, p. 5).

This legislation provides for the long-term stable placement of children removed from, and unable to return to, their families due to child protection concerns – primarily children who have experienced significant abuse and neglect, and disrupted placements. This group of children, which includes older children and those with disabilities, are not available for adoption. A Permanent Care Order grants custody and guardianship to the permanent caregivers until the child is 18 years of age while maintaining the child's legal and social links with their family of origin.

1993: The *Hague Convention on Protection of Children and Co-operation in Respect of Intercountry Adoption* – the ethical/legal instrument which governs the way in which the countries signatory to it deliver (if ratified), or endeavour to deliver, their domestic and intercountry adoption programs – was established.

1995: V.A.N.I.S.H. was asked by the Victorian Government, and subsequently agreed, to extend its search and support services to former state wards and 'careleavers' (now referred to as 'Forgotten Australians'), another group of Victorians who were separated from their families of origin.

1998: The Australian Government ratified the *Hague Convention on Protection of Children and Co-operation in Respect of Intercountry Adoption* (1993).

2001: V.A.N.I.S.H. ceased to be an acronym and was registered as VANISH Inc. in order to include people affected by donor conception and Forgotten Australians under its umbrella.

2005: An Inquiry into the adoption of children from overseas was conducted by the Commonwealth Government House of Representatives Standing Committee on Family and Human Services led by Liberal MP, Bronwyn Bishop. The Committee (House of Representatives Standing Committee on Family and Human Services, 2005, p. viii) found a

> general lack of support for adoption – both local and intercountry – in most of the state and territory welfare departments which are responsible for processing all adoption applications. The lack of support ranged from indifference to hostility, much to the distress of prospective parents seeking to adopt children from overseas.

2006: Amendments were made to the Commonwealth *Family Law Act 1975*, which included a greater emphasis on a child's family and social connections. This was in response to concerns that adoptions by step-parents severed legal ties to the non-custodial parent and extended family; and that adoption by relatives distorted family relationships (for example, by grandparents becoming the legal parents and mothers becoming legal aunts) making it very confusing for the child. Since then, the County Court (of Victoria) must be satisfied that the child's welfare and interests are better served by an adoption order rather than an order for guardianship and custody from the Family Court.

2006: The Victorian government passed the *Charter of Human Rights and Responsibilities Act*, which requires government and public authorities to consider human – including children's – rights when developing laws and policies and delivering services.[7]

2006: VANISH Inc. amended the composition of its Committee of Management to reflect its extension of services to people affected by donor conception.

9 August 2006: Labor Premier Steve Bracks delivered an apology to Forgotten Australians (people who as children spent all or part of their childhood in institutional care across Australia) on behalf of the Victorian Government.

1 January 2008: The Victorian *Charter of Human Rights and Responsibilities Act 2006* came into full effect. With the aim of building a fairer and more inclusive community, this Act gives specific legal protection to 20 fundamental human rights. While it recognises that in certain circumstances some rights may be limited, clear reasons must be provided as to why any such decisions are necessary and reasonable.

13 February 2008: An apology was delivered by Labor Prime Minister Kevin Rudd to the Stolen Generations of Australia's Indigenous peoples.

2008: Deborra-lee Furness launched National Adoption Awareness Week (NAAW)

> to raise the profile of adoption nationwide, to shine a light on the critical issues and shift the anti-adoption culture remaining from the travesties of eras past … Each year, National Adoption Awareness Week (NAAW) occurs across one week in November … (Adopt Change website, 2015).

7 See Victorian Equal Opportunity and Human Rights Commission <http://www.humanrightscommission.vic.gov.au/index.php/about-us >.

Indicative of the way in which the subject of adoption incites strong emotions, polarises public opinion and leaves minimal room for debate, Quartly et al. (2013, p. 1) observed that:

> Some agree with celebrity Deborra-lee Furness that adoption is a legitimate way to form a family, and the best way to relieve the suffering of the more than '100 million orphans in our world'. Others hold that adoption is a crime against mothers and their children that can never be justified.

Until the first half of 2014, the website of NAAW claimed that there were approximately 130 million orphans globally. This was based on a United Nations Children's Fund (UNICEF[8]) calculation, which includes children who have one living parent, as well as those with no living parents (or 'double orphans', as orphans are defined in Australia). The more accurate figure is approximately 13 million (double) orphans globally, most of whom actually reside with extended family members, though this was never acknowledged by NAAW; nor was the fact that the vast majority of children residing in 'orphanages' overseas are placed there by parents/extended family members for reasons of poverty.

16 November 2009: An apology was delivered by Labor Prime Minister Kevin Rudd to the Forgotten Australians and former Child Migrants.

2010: Open Place, a new and separate search and support service for Forgotten Australians, was established with an ongoing relationship with VANISH Inc. through the provision of a family tracing service.

8 UNICEF was established in 1946 as the 'United Nations International Children's Emergency Fund'. Its mandate was subsequently broadened and in 1953, its name shortened to 'United Nations Children's Fund', while its original acronym was retained.

19 October 2010: An apology was delivered by Liberal Premier of Western Australia, Colin Barnett, for past adoption practices.

2012: A review of adoption and permanent care services in Victoria was initiated by DHS in early 2012, scheduled for completion by mid-2013. This was the tenth such review in 20 years. The previous nine reviews were consistently similar in their recommendations to centralise and streamline adoption and permanent care services in Victoria. However, those recommendations were never implemented due to resistance by senior staff in the various agencies long funded to deliver adoption and permanent care services.

18 July 2012: An apology was delivered by Labor Premier of South Australia, Jay Weatherill, for past adoption practices.

14 August 2012: An apology was delivered by Labor Chief Minister of the Australian Capital Territory, Katy Gallagher, for past adoption practices.

20 September 2012: An apology was delivered by Liberal Premier of NSW, Barry O'Farrell, for past adoption practices.

18 October 2012: An apology was delivered by Labor Premier of Tasmania, Lara Giddings, for past adoption practices.

25 October 2012: An apology was delivered by Liberal Premier of Victoria, Ted Baillieu, for past adoption practices.

27 November 2012: An apology was delivered by Liberal National Premier of Queensland, Campbell Newman, for past adoption practices.

21 March 2013: An apology was delivered by Labor Prime Minister Julia Gillard for past adoption practices in Australia.

27 March 2013: Country Liberal Chief Minister of the Northern Territory (NT), Andrew Giles, expressed the NT Government's support for the national apology for past adoption practices delivered on 21 March 2013.

2013: The DHS review of adoption and permanent care services in Victoria remained unfinished at the end of June 2013 and appears to have not been publicly reported on since.

September 2013: Amendments to the *Victorian Adoption Act 1984* were passed by the Napthine Liberal-National Coalition government allowing parents to receive identifying information about their children lost to adoption. The amendments included sanctions against a parent for unwanted contact with their adult adopted child, as indicated by a contact statement which may be registered by the adult adoptee, running counter to the spirit of the Apology for Past Adoption Practices delivered by Liberal Premier Ted Baillieu in October 2012. The amendments also allow a new birth certificate to be issued by *Births Deaths and Marriages* in respect of a child whose adoption was finalised in a *Hague Convention*[9] country with the State's Central Authority involvement.

19 December 2013: New Liberal Prime Minister Tony Abbott announced his intention to make it much easier and faster for Australian citizens to adopt children from overseas.

March 2014: In NSW, sweeping and controversial reforms to the state's child protection system commenced in November 2012 under Family and Community Services Minister Pru Goward. As part of this process, in March 2014, the Liberal-

9 '*Hague Convention*' refers to the *Hague Convention on Protection of Children and Co-operation in Respect of Intercountry Adoption* (1993) to which Australia and the 49 other countries signatory to it (as at 25 July 2015) deliver, or endeavour to deliver, their adoption programs.

National Coalition government passed legislative amendments streamlining and fast-tracking adoptions of children from out-of-home care. The permanent placement principles enshrined in this legislation raise the priority of adoption as the preferred permanent alternative family option for vulnerable children, and make domestic violence a ground for removing newborn babies from their mothers if they do not agree to accept assistance.[10]

April 2014: The Australian Government's *Report of the Interdepartmental Committee on Intercountry Adoption* initiated by Prime Minister Tony Abbott was released. It debunked the myths disseminated by pro-adoption lobbyists regarding the reasons for the increasingly low rates of intercountry adoption in Australia, but nevertheless presented the facts as significant impediments to Australians seeking to adopt children from overseas (*Report of the Interdepartmental Committee on Intercountry Adoption*, 2014, p. vi).

> Given this, there is an imperative to be clear about the impact that any reforms are likely to have on each of these impediments to ensure that expectations of families are realistic with regard to the future of intercountry adoption in Australia, and to make clear that in many cases they will go towards improving the experience of people participating in intercountry adoption rather than making a dramatic change in the rate of adoptions.

Only the first 40 pages of the 320-plus-page report were publicly released: the sections addressing options for reform and subsequent recommendations, possible immediate measures and concluding remarks were withheld.

August 2014: NAAW officially re-launched as Adopt Change.

> The Commonwealth Government of Australia's commitment to adoption reform in December 2013 represented a significant

10 See Needham (2014).

> achievement in the advocacy of NAAW … In 2014, NAAW has officially re-emerged as Adopt Change to allow for always-on, year-round campaigning … (Adopt Change website, 2015).

September 2014: In Victoria, amendments to the *Children, Youth and Families Act 2005* were passed by the Napthine Liberal-National Coalition government to promote planning, decision-making and permanency for vulnerable children and young people. These amendments include the introduction of timelines for earlier consideration of adoption and/or permanent care, following concerns articulated in the findings of the 2012 Protecting Victoria's Vulnerable Children Inquiry report[11] that it takes on average five years to obtain a Permanent Care Order for a child, during which time they are exposed to additional trauma. The purported intent of these amendments is sound. However, it appears contrary to the best interests of vulnerable children; to current departmental practice; and to the intent of the amendments that adoption is listed third in the 'hierarchy of permanency objectives', after family preservation and family reunification, while permanent care is listed fourth. Due to be implemented in March 2016, there has been lobbying by stakeholders to repeal this particular amendment.

October 2014: In NSW, the legislative changes making adoption the preferred placement option for children removed from their families for reasons of child protection (which were passed in March 2014) came into effect.

February 2015: The *Australian Citizenship Amendment (Intercountry Adoption) Bill* was passed, opening the way for expansion and expedition of the existing expatriate pathway for adoption of children overseas by Australians. Expatriate intercountry adoptions occur outside the processing and regulation requirements of the domestic intercountry adoption

11 See Cummins, Scott and Scales (2012).

programs provided by the Australian states and territories. The number of expatriate intercountry adoptions currently exceeds the number of intercountry adoptions conducted through the domestically provided programs and is growing. The new legislation means that children adopted overseas in accordance with a bilateral agreement can now be granted citizenship in the same way as children adopted in accordance with the *Hague Convention*.[12] While this legislation applies only to the two countries currently subject to bilateral agreements with Australia (South Korea and Taiwan), the Commonwealth government is endeavouring to establish bilateral agreements with many more countries. Bilateral agreements do not generally meet the ethical and legal rigour inherent in *Hague Convention* country-to-country or domestic arrangements.

May 2015: The Australian Government launched 'Intercountry Adoption Australia', a national website and a free telephone information line operated by the Department of Social Services "to help Australian families navigate the intercountry adoption process," including guiding them through the process of adopting a child from overseas and connecting them to a range of resources and services. According to Prime Minister Tony Abbott, the "new one-stop-shop will … help Australian families work through what can be a long, frustrating and painful process."[13] The new service is designed to guide people wanting to adopt from overseas while still ensuring intercountry adoption occurs in the best interests of the child; it does not affect the delivery of intercountry adoption programs by the states and territories.[14]

12 Australian Government Attorney-General's Department website, accessed 24 July 2015.

13 See Abbott (2015).

14 Sources: Australian Government websites for the Attorney-General's Department; the Department of Social Services; and Intercountry Adoption Australia.

August 2015: The Victorian Andrews Labor government repealed the legislative amendments to the *Adoption Act 1984* regarding the sanctions for unwanted contact of adult adoptees by their (birth) parents, which had been introduced by the previous (Napthine) government.

The principle of 'best interests of the child' has underpinned adoption legislation in Australia since first introduced over a century ago. Yet, interpretation of that principle and the degree to which adoption policies and practices have favoured the interests of prospective adopting parents have varied enormously, thus contributing to the significant fluctuations in adoption numbers, both domestic and intercountry, over the decades. In recent years, the numbers of adoptions have been persistently low; pro-adoption parties have been increasingly organised and determined in their efforts to reverse this situation; and the principle of 'permanency planning' has gained momentum as the primary vehicle for changing the way in which Australian governments interpret the 'best interests of the child' with a view to 'streamlining' – that is, increasing and expediting – adoptions.

CHAPTER 3

A social worker in intercountry adoption

I was aware from childhood that couples, usually infertile, increasingly adopted children from developing countries when the numbers available domestically decreased dramatically during the 1970s. Even in the small rural town of Buchan South, I knew a local family whose relatives adopted a child from Vietnam.

It was a combination of factors that led me, early in 2002, to apply for a part-time Senior Social Worker position with ICAS – the intercountry adoption program delivered by the Victorian Department of Human Services (DHS, formerly CSV, now DHHS). Firstly, I had developed confidence in my acquired professional knowledge and experience. I figured that nothing could be more difficult professionally than working in the child protection program, or personally than losing my twin babies. Secondly, my personal circumstances had changed. A few years prior I had addressed issues associated with my adoption during the counselling I undertook after my twins died. And now my first child was settling into his second year of primary schooling. Thirdly, the timing was good. As co-founders of a consultancy business that we had run successfully for four-and-a-half years, a close friend and I had recently decided to dissolve our business due to differing family commitments and employment needs. Finally, I had an opportunity. A former colleague from my child protection days advised me of a job vacancy.

I recognised that it was challenging for Mum when I joined ICAS. Whenever we discussed my work, she seemed to feel the need to reiterate how anxious she and Dad had felt throughout the processes associated with the adoptions of my brother and me. Of course, I often saw the same anxiety in applicants to ICAS. I frequently became involved in discussions with Mum about the more rigorous nature of the screening and assessment processes applied to prospective adoptive parents in the context of my work compared with that in the era of my own adoption; the impacts of the multiple losses experienced by the children and subsequent complexity of their needs; and that the *children* were now considered to be the primary clients in adoption, rather than the prospective parents. For the last several of my years at ICAS, until 2013 when I left, we shared office space and some clients with FIND (Family Information Networks and Discovery, formerly known as the Adoption Information Service). So I also often discussed with Mum that many adopted people (including young adults who were adopted from overseas as children), as well as former wards of state and young adults who were donor conceived, sought information about their history and contact with family of origin members.

During my interview for the job with ICAS, I was upfront about my personal experience of adoption. I outlined the challenges I had confronted in my adoption journey and how I had dealt and was still dealing with them; how my lived experiences were both relevant and not relevant to other adoptees' lived experiences; and how I believed I could utilise my professional and personal knowledge, experiences and skills to facilitate my work at ICAS. I was asked whether I believed in intercountry adoption; that is, whether I thought it a good thing. I responded as honestly as I could at the time:

"If intercountry adoption needs to be done, then it needs to be done well."

I worked in a range of roles with ICAS over an almost 12-year period, during which intercountry adoption underwent significant global change. The numbers of children identified as requiring intercountry adoption by the accredited overseas adoption authorities[15] decreased significantly after peaking in the mid-2000s. This was the result of commendable improvements in domestic child support and alternative care programs in the countries of origin – just as had happened previously here in Australia.

As the countries of origin became increasingly effective in finding suitable alternative families for vulnerable children domestically, a significant mismatch developed between the needs of the children identified as requiring overseas adoption and the characteristics of the children Australians wished to adopt. The children identified by their countries of origin are now generally over two years (and frequently over four years) of age and have developmental, psychological, physical and/or medical impairments, and/or significant genetic risk factors – often collectively referred to as 'special needs'. But the children that prospective adoptive parents generally seek are healthy infants.

Meanwhile, self-interested parent groups and pro-adoption lobbyists endeavoured to resist the inevitable decline in the numbers of intercountry adoptions by Australians. As noted by Dr Patricia Fronek and Professor Denise Cuthbert (2013, p. 408):

> Today, Australian social workers and other human services practitioners are subjected to enormous pressure from politicians and lobbying groups promoting the practice of intercountry adoption to reduce waiting times, increase numbers, and find new source countries of children … .

15 'Accredited overseas adoption authorities' means accredited in terms of the *Hague Convention.*

In particular, in 2005 under John Howard's government, Bronwyn Bishop led a Parliamentary Inquiry into Adoption of Children from Overseas. It could well be that Ms Bishop was convinced before commencing her Inquiry that she would find an 'anti-adoption' culture and, if so, her Inquiry delivered a self-fulfilling prophecy. Along with my colleagues, I was appalled by the often highly inaccurate claims made by pro-adoption campaigners and the unfair tactics they utilised. For example, it was concluded in the Report of the Overseas Adoption Inquiry (p. 4) that "adoption is either neglected or some departmental officers are openly hostile to it" on the basis of emotive verbal submissions from a procession of disgruntled adopters and prospective adopters. A state government employee who represented her department's intercountry adoption program during the Inquiry later told me that when making her verbal submission she was treated rudely by some of the Committee members and, especially, by Ms Bishop. She was frequently interrupted and cross-questioned before she had finished answering a given question; was instructed to give simplistic yes/no responses; and generally was not permitted to explain the complex policies and processes involved in intercountry adoption and the reasons for them.

I became increasingly frustrated that employment with DHS meant not being allowed to speak publicly to correct the misinformation disseminated by the pro-adoption parties or to defend the policies and decisions of ICAS staff. For example, it was suggested in the government Report of the Overseas Adoption Inquiry that the policy of the Queensland and Victorian intercountry adoption programs which restricted pregnant women from making application was purely administrative – therefore arbitrary, unreasonable and unenforceable – because it was not backed up by legislation. There was no acknowledgement that, whether imposed by legislation or policy, this requirement was a legitimate factor in an assessment of suitability; or that its purpose was to ensure an applicant family was able to provide sufficient attention and space for each new child entering their family. In turn, this would help avoid competitiveness between children (who might otherwise join the family at the same time) for attention from the adoptive parents; assist the attachment of the adopted child and his or her new parents to each other; and thus facilitate a positive outcome for the adoptive placement. I was also annoyed that senior management did not take a more assertive stance in correcting such misguided understandings, and that the pro-adoption lobbyists took full advantage of this. For example, mainstream newspapers quoted the lobbyists' claims that social workers' enforcement of the pregnancy policy was 'invasive', implying that it discriminated against pregnant women, and DHS would make no public comment.

Contrary to the assumption that there existed an 'anti-adoption' culture among social workers delivering adoption programs, I had reached the conclusion that the fact that adoption was still considered by some to hold an important place in child welfare policy was more indicative of the continuing existence of a pro-adoption culture among a small but influential group of social workers in the adoption and permanent care sector in Victoria. Further, it was evident to me that an even more influential 'anti-social worker' culture existed among prospective/adoptive parents, pro-adoption advocates and politicians. As Fronek and Cuthbert (2013, p. 408) have noted:

> Increasingly, social workers are marginalised in … political and legal negotiations which often gain media attention and scrutiny. It could be argued that this marginalisation is consequent to the deprofessionalisation of social work beginning in the 1990s and the expanded role of the federal government following the 2005 inquiry into adoption … .

This realisation was associated with feeling strangely doomed to vicariously relive my unremembered – yet unforgotten – experience of being a helpless voiceless baby about whom decisions were made for the future with no one advocating for my rights.

In any event, as the numbers of healthy infants requiring intercountry adoption declined, the waiting times for applicants to be matched with a child (a process that occurs in the countries of origin) after ICAS approval also stretched out, doubling in length, sometimes tripling to ten years or even more. ICAS responded by restricting the number and nature of new applications lodged to only those that the overseas countries were specifically seeking – a major change from the previous continuous processing model. ICAS increasingly adapted to becoming a special needs only program. This included introducing a pre-entry waiting list; revamping the applicant information and education processes; more vigorously encouraging applicants to consider applying for permanent care, in particular, or local adoption, though this was rarely considered in the best interests of a child; and increasing contact with and support of applicants, both pre- and post-placement. Prospective adopters waiting to be matched with healthy infants – particularly from China, which had been the biggest and most expedient program – progressively withdrew their applications or had them mandatorily closed by ICAS staff in significant numbers. Subsequently, several such former ICAS applicants sought to parent vulnerable children via their respective local Adoption and Permanent Care program, and many of them succeeded in being placed with a child on a Permanent Care Order. Others moved overseas with their employment for a period in order to be eligible to adopt children as expatriate Australians, or sought children through overseas commercial surrogacy practices – often without advising ICAS and withdrawing their adoption applications first.

I was by no means the only ICAS Senior Social Worker to discover multiple cases in which applicants had a new child – either through birth, expatriate adoption, or overseas surrogacy – only upon initiating their mandatory two-year re-assessment process. Despite having signed written agreements at the beginning of the application process that they would advise ICAS immediately if they became pregnant or a child joined their family via other means, the new parents were invariably surprised – and not infrequently also angry – that they were not permitted to continue with their ICAS application. They often denied that the arrival of a new child was a significant change in their family's circumstances. Or they suddenly disagreed with the requirements for a minimum two-year gap between both the age and arrival of the youngest/newest existing child in their family and any future adopted child.

During my years with ICAS, I met and worked with some wonderful prospective and adoptive families who understood, or came to understand, that intercountry adoption – even of an apparently healthy infant – necessarily involves trauma and losses for the child that will have significant long-term ramifications for their behaviour and well-being. I have every confidence that the children adopted by those families will achieve as much of their potential and be as happy throughout their lives as is possible under the circumstances – that is, given their exceptionally difficult starts in life and that they were intercountry adopted.

However, also during my time with ICAS, I experienced the attitudes of many prospective and adoptive parents as increasingly demanding, unreasonable, critical and blaming of ICAS staff – as if it was ICAS's fault they did not have a child; as if ICAS was deliberately hindering or stopping them from having a child. Even when matched or sometimes even placed with a child, applicants increasingly complained that the characteristics of the child were more complex than they had sought. In fact, non-acceptance of child placement proposals by applicants approved to adopt children with complex or special needs increased dramatically between 2009 and 2013. Applicants also complained that this was ICAS's fault. They even complained that requests to comply with ICAS policies (for example, delaying the timing of enrolment at childcare/kinder/school in order to facilitate development of the child's attachment with his or her new parents) to which they had previously indicated understanding and written agreement were now unreasonable. While the number of active ICAS applications decreased significantly, the rate of complaints increased. High emotions, particularly frustration and anger, were directed by applicants onto ICAS staff members through venomous comments and accusations – disguised thinly or, sometimes, not at all – in angry letters to ICAS management and the Minister for Community Services; posts on intercountry adoption support group websites; and verbal interactions during phone conversations and office interviews.

I certainly received my share of personal criticism and vitriol from ICAS applicants. For example, in two phone conversations, different male applicants threatened to contact their 'close friend' – one a senior government minister and the other a senior bureaucrat in other State Government Departments – to complain about and overrule me because I would not recommend re-approval of their respective applications unless they could agree to abide by specific ICAS policies (developed from research and practice wisdom on the basis of being in the best interests of the adopted child, and mandatory for all ICAS applicants). On another occasion, a female applicant verbally abused me for some 40 minutes on the phone, angry that she and her husband had already been waiting four years to be matched with a child through a very small program in a particular country (the only country to which they wished to apply) and I was unable to confirm when, or even if, they might be matched. Further, in response to a 20-page assessment report in which the assessing social worker and I, the supervising Senior Social Worker, raised a number of issues regarding her and her husband's application, another female applicant wrote a 30-page letter detailing what appeared to be every grievance she had ever had about ICAS staff but had not previously raised with us.

But by far the most frustrating and demoralising interactions from my point of view occurred during applicant education sessions – conducted after the applicants had been successfully screened, but before they had completed lodgement of their full applications. Particularly during my last years with ICAS in 2012 and 2013 – during which time only applications from people seeking to adopt a child with special needs were accepted – I was sometimes asked to present to applicants from my perspective as an adoptee on the ICAS policy (strongly recommended, though not legally enforceable) requiring adoptive parents to not change their adopted child's name. The rationale behind this policy is that it enables the child to maintain one of the very few things he or she is able to bring with them from their country of origin – their identity. Yet, even applicants who otherwise seemed to understand that intercountry adopted children will have suffered significant losses and trauma (both by the time they are identified as requiring overseas adoption and, further, as a result of subsequently being adopted by an overseas family) would often argue against this policy. They invariably cited that they had for years had their heart set on a favourite name picked out for their future child, perhaps a popular name or one derived from their own family history. This was something I understood intimately from the experience of my own adoptive parents' re-naming of me when it was considered a healthy part of the process of the adoptive parents 'claiming' their adopted child. It was as if everyone anticipated that a future adopted child could simply replace the biological child the adoptive parents would never have; as if the adopted child had been born to them.

Some applicants also argued that their parents, who were immigrants, had chosen anglicised names for them and their siblings born in Australia; or that they, as immigrants themselves, had chosen to anglicise their own names on arrival here. The applicants who maintained that they did not wish to test their fertility were sometimes even more resistant to accepting the ICAS child name policy than applicants who had previously undergone years of unsuccessful IVF treatment. Their attitude seemed to be that, as 'altruistic adopters', they were more entitled than most adoptive parents to change their child's name.

I tried my best to communicate to the applicants that the name changes they were comparing had been decisions made for them either by themselves or by their biological parents who had cared for them continuously since birth, and that the situation was very different for an intercountry adopted child. Even sharing my personal ongoing hurt since discovering as a young adult that my adoptive parents changed my original name had little impact on convincing applicants that changing their adopted child's name would exacerbate identity and trust issues for the child; and that, by the time their adopted child reached adulthood, he or she would not necessarily be grateful to them for the 'gift' of a new name. Most of the applicants argued that their adopted child could choose whether they wanted to change their name back to their original name when they turned 18. They could not see the unfairness of the onus being placed on the child to reclaim their lost identity, particularly when it was so simple for the adoptive parents to maintain the child's existing name in the first place.

I also tried my best to separate the personal from the professional. Ultimately, however, part of my experience of the applicants' fierce resistance to the ICAS child name policy was a denial of my own lived experience as an adoptee, as well as an arbitrary dismissal of my many years of professional social work knowledge and experience in relation to vulnerable children in out-of-home care and the aftermath of their lived experiences. One applicant (a non-welfare trained small business owner) even told me that the research on which much

ICAS policy and practice was based originated from the field of psychology and could thus be dismissed, as psychology was such a 'new' profession.

All of this was consistent with what I had observed over several years – perhaps over my entire lifetime – that the vast majority of prospective adoptive parents primarily seek a child to fulfil their own needs, not to fulfil the child's needs, despite the fact they may firmly believe their personal motivations are genuinely altruistic.

Further, it was amply evident to me that adoptive applicants are generally able to take in only a relatively small proportion of the information provided to them about the complexities of adoption through the application processes, tending to retain only what they want to hear about it. Adoption applicants – and pro-adoption lobbyists alike – predominantly want to hear only about the aspects associated with their own happiness, not about the aspects associated with the adopted child's losses and trauma. But the sad truth is that adoptive parents cannot experience their happiness without the child experiencing losses and trauma, regardless of how well they love and parent the child. A materially affluent lifestyle can never fully compensate for the losses of identity, primary and extended family relationships, and language, culture and country of origin that the adopted child will also inevitably experience.

Similarly, in regard to the relatively few people who expressed a wish to adopt children with significant special needs – children who may never be able to develop verbal skills in their native language, let alone in English, and/or who have mobility challenges such that they will require intensive physical care and health services for their entire lives – I came to the view that those prospective parents generally believed the children's disabilities were 'fixable', or at least highly improvable, with the intensive service provision and nurturing family life they anticipated they would be able to provide. These people often significantly underrated the parenting challenges involved and were overly optimistic about the rewards for themselves associated with parenting such children. They were naively dismissive of both the negatives of intercountry adoption for such children, and the capacity of overseas child welfare agencies to cater for the needs of children with special needs if they did not also have to accommodate the numerous 'healthy' children placed in their centres by families experiencing poverty. Non-disabled intercountry adopted children have a huge challenge learning the English language, which compounds the additional challenge of communicating their complex emotions and feelings with their immature age-related conceptual abilities. It would be naïve to assume that disabled intercountry adopted children, especially those without the capacity to learn expressive English skills, would experience less significant trauma and loss than other intercountry adopted children simply because they were unable to communicate it verbally.

Prospective parents seeking to adopt disabled intercountry children were often themselves significantly older than other prospective parents. Hence, I also felt uncomfortable regarding the expectations of such applicants to be able to remove disabled children from the country in which they were born and lived for some years, only to inflict further losses and grief on the children when they – the adoptive parents – died. Was it fair to do this to the children, taking advantage of their inability to communicate their wishes and emotional pain? Was it fair for adoptive parents to bequeath the care of such children to their existing biological teenaged or adult children? Or, if they had no other children, to their extended family members? Or, if they had no extended family members able or willing to take on the care of the adopted children, on the alternative care services provided through the state from taxpayer funds? Many parents of significantly disabled children born to them here would argue that there are insufficient health, respite and allied services available to adequately assist and support them in Victoria – indeed, in Australia – to meet their children's lifelong needs. After all, the National Disability Insurance Scheme is still in its infancy and yet to prove whether it can live up to its intended aims.

During my time with ICAS we had three managers and under each of them we attempted to change the name of our program. 'ICAS' is the acronym for 'Inter-Country Adoption Service'. We staff wanted to change the name to something like 'Intercountry Adoption Program', so long as the word 'service' was either replaced with 'program' or removed altogether. After all, we were very clear that the purpose of our program was to find suitable families for the vulnerable children identified by their countries of origin as being in need of intercountry adoption as a last resort. We felt that prospective adoptive parents often approached ICAS with inappropriate views. For example, they seemed to think we were providing a family formation *service* for them, rather than being an alternative family *program* for vulnerable overseas children. The applicants expected to be treated as if they were the primary clients, not the children. They also acted like they had a right to adopt an intercountry child, rather than a *responsibility* to be screened and assessed for suitability to adopt an intercountry child.

It seemed such a simple thing – for our program name to be more accurate and thus to appropriately orient applicant expectations. It also seemed especially important, given our practical experience that the vast majority of people who expressed interest in adopting intercountry children were not suitable. This was evidenced by the high rates of self-selection out of the application process from the point of initial enquiry through to assessment and, ultimately, placement. It was also evidenced by the nature of many of the phone enquiries received by ICAS through our daily duty service. Even when ICAS was placing as many as 100 or more intercountry children per year, we regularly received phone enquiries from prospective parents seeking to adopt an 'orphan' the day after a natural disaster occurred in a developing country (such as an earthquake, tsunami or famine). Often such enquirers refused to believe that disaster response agencies recommended strongly against removing child survivors from their communities immediately after such events, in order to facilitate reunification efforts for the children with surviving extended family members and minimise further trauma to the children. They would also often become angry, as they wrongly perceived that ICAS staff were deliberately thwarting their altruistic endeavours to care for a needy child from an impoverished Third World country.

Yet, senior DHS management and the Minister for Community Services failed to approve our request for a program name change on each occasion that we raised it. Such were the politics and sensitivities associated with intercountry adoption specifically, but also with adoption generally. In fact, I had experienced a similar situation with DHS management years earlier in relation to an adoption project for which I was commissioned as an external consultant. The project involved producing an adoption information book for use by practitioners in the health and welfare fields. The target practitioners were primarily in counselling roles. They worked with children and families and their clients often included individuals who were party to an adoption or permanent care placement. The primary purpose of the book was to supplement the knowledge base of practitioners regarding the issues, needs and challenges of individuals involved in adoption and permanent care placements; and to enhance sensitivity, support and effectiveness in providing services to such individuals. The project commenced in 1998 and was finalised in 2000.

The 80-page document had to be approved by senior management and the minister before it could be printed and distributed to the target service providers. However, this approval was never given, despite recognition by the relevant DHS program staff that it would meet an information gap clearly identified by the practitioners themselves. The book had been thoroughly researched and it was well received by the few practitioners who were invited to review it and provide feedback. However, it was considered too controversial – 'too negative' – by senior DHS managers and the minister.

By mid-2012 when DHS commenced its tenth review of the state's adoption and permanent care services in some 20 years, on average around 20 children were being placed for adoption each in the local infant adoption and ICAS programs annually; while the number of Permanent Care Orders being granted was around 250 and increasing.[16] I thus anticipated the review would recommend that ICAS should either be phased out altogether or become fully integrated into the local out-of-home care system. Given that I considered either option would have been an appropriate outcome, I figured I would be able to cope with my growing unease till then. However, the review was subsequently extended, then apparently placed on hold. As far as I am aware at the time of writing in August 2015, there has still been no specific report or documented outcomes publicly distributed from the review. Yet, amendments to the *Children, Youth and Families Act* – including amendments pertaining to adoption and permanent care – were approved by the Victorian parliament in September 2014.

On 2 October 2013, I attended a panel discussion, 'Surrogacy and adoption: Pitfalls and promises', featuring Chief Judge John Pascoe, Professor Nahum Mushin and Professor Denise Cuthbert. I heard nothing I had not read or discussed with my ICAS colleagues previously. However, on hearing it presented all together I was struck by how, even when done well, the long term negatives associated with intercountry adoption greatly outweighed the short term positives; and how there were better, more cost-effective, means by which suitable families

16 Australian Institute of Health and Welfare (2013) 'Adoptions Australia 2012-13' Child Welfare Series No. 57, Australian Government, Canberra <http://www.aihw.gov.au/WorkArea/DownloadAsset.aspx?id=60129545513>.

could be found for vulnerable children in their countries of birth. In the words of Fronek and Cuthbert (2013, p. 407):

> Some intercountry adoption scholars have proposed on multiple occasions that if the money invested into intercountry adoption was invested into community development that strengthened families and communities, different outcomes would be achieved and the impact of inequality and poverty would be alleviated … Confronting the powerful vested interests in the adoption industry, and in parent organisations that use the media to advance their interests in accessing greater numbers of children with fewer impediments (usually framed as red tape or bureaucracy) for adoption is … necessary.

The panel discussion also confirmed for me that, given the significant decrease in the numbers of children available through the regulated intercountry adoption pathway, overseas expatriate adoption and commercial surrogacy were increasingly providing the next unregulated markets for desperate prospective Australian parents to exploit in procuring children. I found this an abominable situation.

I needed to debrief and found myself talking afterwards with a group of women from ARMS (the Australian Relinquishing Mothers Society) – they even gave me a lift home. So moved by the realisation that adoption rarely 'needs' to be done – if at all – any more, I felt unable to continue working at ICAS and tendered my resignation on principle the following day. However, I was persuaded to stay on until the end of December 2013 to progress some clinical data mining research I had initiated in 2012 regarding ICAS applications for children with additional special needs.

On 12 November 2013, the appropriateness of my decision to resign from ICAS was vindicated when I attended another panel discussion. This one was primarily focused on intercountry adoption, 'Forming Families: National Adoption Awareness

Week (NAAW)'[17] – NAAW being the pro-adoption campaign organisation founded by expatriate Australian celebrity adoption lobbyist, Deborra-lee Furness, in 2008. (NAAW was re-launched as 'Adopt Change' in August 2014.) I was appalled that neither Ms Furness nor the other guest speaker, American Dr Jane Aronson, referred even once during the hour-long session to the *Hague Convention on Protection of Children and Co-operation in Respect of Intercountry Adoption.* I sought an explanation for this during question-and-answer time at the end of the panel presentation. Dr Aronson responded that the omission was 'deliberate'. I also sought clarification from Ms Furness as to why she continues to erroneously assert that the reason for the decline in intercountry adoptions is due to an 'anti-adoption culture' among the social workers delivering the programs when, as a social worker with ICAS, I knew for a fact that this was not true. Ms Furness responded that it was not her who found the 'anti-adoption culture', rather it was Bronwyn Bishop during her 2005 Inquiry!

As observed by other intercountry adoption commentators, I was well aware that "Deborra-lee Furness is only the most recent in a long line of adopting parents to condemn what they see as an anti-adoption culture in Australia" and that "media reports have consistently supported the parents' claim that policy-makers and social welfare practitioners are hostile towards adoption – and especially intercountry adoption" (Quartly et al., 2013, p. 120). I was nevertheless disappointed and disturbed to witness first-hand Ms Furness dodging ownership of her opinion when challenged, and Dr Aronson intentionally avoiding discussion of the importance of the *Hague Convention* designed to safeguard the best interests of children and their families of origin in matters pertaining to intercountry adoption. I recognised that, for both speakers,

17 This panel discussion, including questions and answers, was filmed and is available online <http://wheelercentre.com/videos/video/the-fifth-estate-forming-families-national-adoption-awareness-week/>.

their frame of reference (both their physical home and the metaphorical home to their ideal adoption model) was the USA – a country with a long history of unregulated adoption practices outside the safeguards and requirements of the *Hague Convention* which the USA had only recently decided to ratify.

There were other things that left me less than impressed with that panel discussion. For example, during question-and-answer time Ms Furness greeted the Manager of VANISH, Coleen Clare, when the latter rose to seek the panel's response on the need for adopted children to maintain links with their family of origin members, as if Ms Clare were an enthusiastic new recruit to the NAAW mission. This was based on Ms Clare having accepted an invitation to attend a dinner hosted by NAAW the previous evening, despite Ms Clare having repeatedly challenged the pro-adoption stance of Ms Furness during that dinner, drawing on VANISH's 25 years of direct learning from working with adult people who were themselves adopted.

Further, Ms Furness boasted that NAAW had received a one million dollar donation from James Packer and another significant, although undisclosed, sum from the Pratt Foundation in order to 'write policy' on adoption for the Australian Government. As a government employee and consultant for most of my social work career, I had always considered it best practice for policy in the field of children's and family services to be developed by impartial government staff with relevant expertise and in consultation with all relevant parties – not just self-interested lobby groups. I had difficulty believing that any responsible government would permit a lobbyist with no professional expertise in the field to determine its policy in an area as complex as adoption. On the other hand, I had an inkling even then that "Lobbying is a lucrative industry with scant regulation where the line between lobbyist and politician is becoming increasingly blurred."[18]

18 Editorial opinion in *The Saturday Paper* (2015).

Still, I also had difficulty digesting that Ms Furness had managed to secure a massive financial donation from the Pratt Foundation, a major philanthropic source in Victoria, for the purposes of pursuing a campaign to permanently separate children from their families, rather than for the purposes of providing a service to support children and their families to remain together either overseas or within Australia.

It was after that panel discussion but before I had finished up working with ICAS at the end of December 2013 that I came across an article brimming with simplistic, emotive and unsubstantiated assertions by Ms Furness in a 2011 publication (Jackman, 2011, pp. 42–43). It said: "In Australia, there are many families who would desperately love to provide ... care [to the millions of orphans and unwanted children] but they are being stopped by the system." There was no acknowledgement that not everyone who expresses a wish to adopt a child from overseas will be suitable. Here is a second example: "The process is ... very invasive and intrusive in the way potential adoptive parents are put through the wringer in regards to their personal life. From every account, their treatment was far from kind or supportive." There was no acknowledgement that the comprehensive screening and assessment processes involved are necessary to prevent prospective adopters with inappropriate motivations (e.g. paedophilia) and unsuitable circumstances (e.g. a criminal record for domestic violence) from adopting. Or that it is essential to be thorough in assessing applicants, given that the act of losing their family, country, culture, language, name and identity for the purposes of intercountry adoption will further traumatise a vulnerable child from overseas. Or that desperate prospective adopters feel very sensitive and often project onto others their perception that any delay in obtaining a child is a deliberate hurdle. Here is a final example: "Ordinary Australians are probably not aware of how unjust and dire the intercountry adoption program in this country is." There was no acknowledgement that most welfare professionals view the decrease in intercountry adoptions as indicative of positive developments for vulnerable children in their countries of origin. The article went on to outline Ms Furness's personal blueprint for 'fixing' intercountry adoption policy in Australia, which I realised was destined to form the basis of the adoption policy she had avowed to write for the government.

I found it difficult to believe that such an attitude of entitlement to adopt an intercountry child could have co-existed in the same space as work towards a national apology for the poor and unethical domestic adoption practices of Australia's past.

CHAPTER 4

Apology or hypocrisy?

In November 2010, the Australian Senate referred to its Community Affairs References Committee an inquiry into former forced adoption policies and practices. This was in response to increasing pressure from widespread activism by adoption stakeholders around Australia over many years, as evidenced by the parliamentary inquiries into past adoption practices conducted in NSW from 1998 and Tasmania from 1999. While no such parliamentary inquiry had been conducted in Western Australia, that state was the first and, at the time, only one to have formally apologised to women, their children and families affected by past forced adoption practices. The Western Australian apology was delivered the month prior to the announcement of the Australian Senate inquiry into former forced adoption policies and practices.

It was originally intended that the Senate Committee would report its findings by the end of June 2011. However, due to the large volume of submissions and the complexity of the subject, the Committee sought extensions for its work, initially to November 2011 and then to February 2012. The Committee delivered its Report, *Commonwealth Contribution to Former Forced Adoption Policies and Practices* (February 2012), subsequent to which the Australian Government announced in June 2012 that it intended to issue a national apology to those affected by forced adoption practices. A Reference Group was established to provide advice on the wording, timing and delivery of the apology.

In August 2012, Australian adoption researchers wrote to Professor Nahum Mushin, the Chair of the Reference Group for the national apology, proposing that it should be explicitly extended to those affected by forced adoption practices in intercountry adoption (Fronek and Cuthbert, 2013, p. 402). On 25 November 2012, an article published in *The Age* newspaper (Han, 2012) detailed how, in conjunction with the adoption researchers and adoptee support groups, young adult Australians adopted as children from South Korea were "calling on the federal government to recognise the suffering of overseas birth mothers and their children in its impending apology for domestic forced adoption practices." Case examples were cited which demonstrated that "many intercountry adoptions were also characterised by coercion and deception, and that the government failed to prevent overseas children being removed in conditions it was opposed to in Australia" (Han, 2012).

On 21 March 2013, Labor Prime Minister Julia Gillard made the anticipated national apology to the thousands of Australians affected by unethical and forced adoptions. There is no way to reliably calculate the number of adoptions in Australia since the 1920s, but it has been estimated that there were as many as 250,000 adoptions during this period.[19] The full transcript is included in Appendix I, but a brief excerpt follows to indicate the gist and importance of the apology speech (Gillard, 2013):[20]

> We offer this apology in the hope that it will assist your healing and in order to shine a light on a dark period of our nation's history …
>
> We resolve, as a nation, to do all in our power to make sure these practices are never repeated. In facing future challenges, we

19 See Higgins (2010).

20 Refer to Appendix I for the full transcript of Prime Minister Gillard's apology speech (2013).

> will remember the lessons of family separation. Our focus will be on protecting the fundamental rights of children and on the importance of the child's right to know and be cared for by his or her parents.

Ms Gillard's speech, lauded as perhaps her finest, was received emotionally and with a standing ovation from those who attended the Great Hall of Parliament House in Canberra to hear it. I watched it delivered live on television by myself at home – it was one of my non-work days. I was also moved to tears. The Prime Minister's words affirmed the often invisible complexities and inherent pain of my own experiences, and reassured me that there was now recognition at the national – the highest – level that forced and closed adoptions should never be allowed to happen again in Australia. Ms Gillard's speech was compared favourably in the media with former Labor Prime Minister Kevin Rudd's finest speech in that role – the national apology made in 2008 for Australia's Stolen Generations of Indigenous people, many of whom were adopted after forced separation from their families of origin. In 2009, as Opposition spokesperson for Indigenous affairs, Tony Abbott admitted that the Coalition had made a mistake by refusing to apologise to Australia's Indigenous population.

On 21 March 2013, Opposition Leader Tony Abbott also gave a speech.[21] I had turned the television off directly after Ms Gillard spoke, and thus did not hear it delivered live. However, my subsequent reading of and written media reports about it (for example, David Wroe and Tony Wright, 2013) indicate that Mr Abbott's speech was poor in comparison to the Prime Minister's; that it reflected a lack of understanding regarding the key issues and sensitivities involved; and that it was interrupted by several women in the audience who

21 The full transcript of Tony Abbott's apology speech is provided in Appendix II.

objected to his use of the term 'birth parents', one of whom requested that he retract it. Still, I had no reason to believe that Tony Abbott's apparently confused perspective in relation to adoption would have any bearing on adoption policy in Australia in the immediate future.

Unfortunately, Prime Minister Gillard's apology speech was "quickly overwhelmed by a bitter challenge to [her] leadership" later the same day (*The Drum*, 2013). Inordinate excitement was generated in the media in response to the attempted leadership spill within the Labor caucus. This excitement was sustained until the federal election that took place six months later, and effectively diverted attention away from – and undermined – the significance of the national adoption apology. In fact, reporting on the negatives associated with adoption was dumped by the mainstream Australian media and thus also from the consciousness of the broader Australian community.

On 19 December 2013, new Liberal Prime Minister Tony Abbott (who had been elected in September 2013) announced his commitment to making intercountry adoption "much easier and faster for Australian couples." Mr Abbott stated, "For too long, adoption has been in the too-hard basket … For too long it has been a policy no-go zone … That must change … and it will change within 12 months." He announced the establishment of a Commonwealth Interdepartmental Committee on Overseas Adoption to report to him on 'reform' of Australia's intercountry adoption program and subsequently inform discussion at the next COAG (Council of Australian Governments) meeting to be held approximately five months' hence. "The committee will consult extensively," he said. "I do not underestimate the complexity of the work to be undertaken in this area. I recognise the need to have a broad and inclusive discussion about proposed change to ensure that, as a community, we do not repeat the mistakes of the past …" (Swan, 2013).

I was truly shocked and distressed when I saw footage of Tony Abbott making his announcement about 'reforming' intercountry adoption on the evening news. I was numb with disbelief. Had he not earlier the very same year, when Leader of the Opposition, given bi-partisan support to Prime Minister Julia Gillard's national apology to those affected by the misguided pre-1980s policies and practices of adoption in Australia? Had he not then stated "there are big lessons here, now and for the future … part of apologising for old mistakes is striving to avoid new ones"? Were the words of the new Prime Minister merely a figment of my excitable imagination? Or was Tony Abbott one of the most brazenly hypocritical politicians in Australia's history? Perhaps, in fact, he was just being true to type. After all, as Fronek and Cuthbert have observed: "Generally, intercountry adoptions thrive when political perspectives are neoliberal and free market approaches are favoured …" (2013, p. 409).

In truth, the surprise was probably more that I found myself so shocked by this unexpected development than by the development itself. Yet, I could not suppress my bitter disappointment. I felt as if the national apology, as well as the Victorian government's apology in October 2012, for past unethical adoptions had never actually happened. I felt as if all the personal testimonies and research and effort involved had, in one brief photo opportunity, been unceremoniously unheard, unravelled and undermined. I felt as if *I* had been unravelled and undermined. I was deeply hurt. All the healing I had experienced as a result of the apologies dissipated so quickly and completely that I felt like my old wounds were not only inflamed, but that I had new wounds as well. And I thought I already had enough to deal with in relation to getting through another Christmas – this one was already well and truly ruined.

I felt particularly aggrieved with the televised images of Mr Abbott rubbing elbows with Ms Furness – along with her movie star husband Hugh Jackman, and champion Australian cyclist Cadel Evans (and his wife Chiara Passerini[22]) who adopted a child from Ethiopia as an expatriate Australian. The public announcement was made during a media-friendly gathering at the Prime Minister's formal residence, Kirribilli House in Sydney. To me this provided evidence that Mr Abbott had done a complete U-turn on adoption policy since the National Apology for Forced Adoptions. It was evidence that he had willingly shunned the expert advice of long-term professionals, researchers and academics engaged in the adoption field in Australia. It also provided evidence that he had willingly shunned the lived experiences of adopted people, including intercountry adoptees, and their families of origin. It seemed to prove that Mr Abbott had already embraced the privately well-funded NAAW campaign; that he had already decided to pursue Ms Furness's tunnel-visioned agenda; and that his announcement about establishment of the Commonwealth Interdepartmental Committee on Overseas Adoption was a tokenistic measure designed to make it appear that there was public consultation while in reality it was just going through the motions. "Broad and inclusive discussion," I doubted very much! "For too long ..." he said. What? Nine months was too long for him to soothe the wounds of the previous generations separated from their families by poor adoption policies and practices before creating a new one? Or was he so naïve in relation to adoption issues that he had simply allowed himself to be captured by Ms Furness's celebrity status?

I understood – as expertly documented in the final and, arguably, most important of several significant publications to come out of the four-year national project on the history of adoption in Australia funded by the Australian Research Council and undertaken by Monash University – that

22 Evans and Passerini have since separated, as publicly announced in May 2015 (see Geary, 2015).

Ms Furness's position on adoption was the one generally accepted within Australia by welfare and health professionals, ministers of religion, politicians and editors of women's magazines alike *half a century ago* (Quartly et al., 2013, p. 1):

> Couples who couldn't have children could solve their infertility problem by adopting a baby to rear as if it was their own ... Infertile couples strongly supported this way of thinking ... Mothers and babies were not consulted; it was assumed that their elders knew best.

The Abbott government was already widely known for its denial of facts. For example: its stubborn refusal to acknowledge the extensive scientific evidence and convergence of expert opinion indicating global climate change, and its fierce denial that asylum seekers who arrive by boat are committing no crime and that detaining such refugees offshore is not only a violation of their human rights but akin to torture. Still, had not Mr Abbott previously accepted the evidence relating to adoption which had led to the state and federal apologies? How could anyone change their position so quickly on adoption policy when there was no new evidence contradicting their previous and very publicly held position? How could anyone sincerely believe that re-orienting intercountry adoption as a service for prospective adoptive parents and revamping it as an easier and faster means to create a family could improve the plight of vulnerable children? Oh, but of course. It is not about the children. For the likes of this government, children are just another commodity in the global free market.

I further realised that the opportunity for self-interested lobbyists to gain inordinate power had been created through the Liberal-National Coalition parties having been elected at both federal and state levels. They had subsequently decimated the ranks of experienced human services policy developers within their respective governments under the guise of 'minimising red tape and increasing efficiency'. In fact, Mr Abbott's U-turn on adoption policy is a perfect example of social policy creation under neo-liberal ideology – in the context of a disturbing vacuum of social justice and humanitarian ethics and values.

CHAPTER 5

A campaign

Introduction

I was so thoroughly dismayed and disgusted with Tony Abbott's evident hypocrisy in relation to adoption and the pro-adoption campaign by Deborra-lee Furness that I felt compelled to respond publicly somehow. The first thing that sprang to mind was to send that very evening a several page email to a political journalist based in Canberra whose article I had read on Mr Abbott's 19 December 2013 announcement. I did not receive a reply, not even an acknowledgement that it had been received. No matter. Inspired by Tom Wills – the key and highly-misunderstood figure in the development of Australian football in the mid-1800s[23] – that email marked the pivotal first of many I have written since, especially to the media.

I was determined to defend the achievements of the adoption reformers of the 1970s and 1980s in Victoria – they had introduced Permanent Care Orders and rightly relegated adoption to the option of last resort for vulnerable children. I was resolute in my determination to fight in order to hold

23 I confess that I am passionate about Australian football and, especially, about Melbourne Football Club – the founding football club in Australia. I co-wrote a book on my love of the game, *Real Women Love Footy* (2013); and recently wrote a manuscript for a novel about Tom Wills.

onto this hard-won ground. I knew, both professionally and personally, that permanent care was a far better option than adoption for achieving the best interests of children in the long-term. This was the case irrespective of any institutionalised failings of best practice implementation through lack of adequate dedicated ongoing post-placement funding. I vowed that I would advocate for the rights of the children; that I would wage a campaign against the retrograde neo-liberal movement pressing for the renaissance of adoption in whatever ways I reasonably could – particularly via print.

On 4 February 2014, *Family Confidential* on *ABC1* featured Deborra-lee Furness and her husband, Hugh Jackman: Australian expatriates living primarily in New York where they adopted two children domestically. The program showed the couple attending the birth of one of their children. It did not explain that the USA has long had a privatised and unregulated adoption system. Nor did it explain that the practice of adoptive parents attending the birth of their prospective adopted child is considered coercive, exploitative and unethical in Australia. In fact, this practice is illegal in Australia, as it does not allow for the 'relinquishing' mother – at her most vulnerable during and just after childbirth – the opportunity to privately meet and hold the baby she is contemplating giving up or indeed to reflect upon or reconsider her decision free of distraction or pressure during the legal cooling-off period. But in *Family Confidential*, the prospective parents rush to cut the umbilical cord, apparently ignorant of the precious opportunity their presence denies the mother with her own child. I emailed *The Age* about this. I also argued that the *Family Confidential* program highlighted the misguided nature of Prime Minister Abbott's intention to make adoption of children from overseas easier and faster for prospective Australian parents on the strength of Ms Furness's 'heart-led' campaign, which inordinately favours the interests of prospective adoptive parents over those of vulnerable children and their birth families. My letter was not published. It was thus clear to me from the outset that my campaign would not be an easy one. But nothing could stop me; I had to give it a go!

5.1 Newspapers

5.1.1 Intercountry adoption

On 23 December 2013, *The Age* published an editorial supporting the Prime Minister's intention to 'reform' intercountry adoption. It echoed negative myths about the way in which the state and territory-based intercountry adoption programs have been delivered in Australia – as purported by Ms Furness and NAAW – as if they were facts. I was appalled. *The Age* had long been the only mainstream Australian newspaper I considered worth reading from a social justice and humanitarian perspective, and now it had apparently taken a stance against the rights of a significant group of vulnerable children and their families. I knew I was not alone in strongly suspecting that Ms Furness and Mr Abbott's agenda for intercountry adoption was the thin end of the wedge. It was likely that moves would be made to extend to other states and territories the changes occurring in NSW under its Liberal-National Coalition government and Minister for Family and Community Services, Pru Goward. This would force children residing in temporary out-of-home care placements following removal from their own families through the child protection system into adoption. Thus, I emailed an opinion piece to *The Age* outlining my perspective. So began my campaign to modify the views of that newspaper on the topic of adoption.

I received a courteous reply the same afternoon advising me they would not be able to find space for it, "important though the subject matter is." I responded, communicating my hope that *The Age* would give further attention to this matter from the perspectives of adult intercountry adoptees and local adoption experts, as well as that of adoptive parents and adoption advocates.

And I kept writing. My first success was with a letter that I emailed on Christmas Eve.

Published in *The Age*, Thursday, 26 December 2013

The forgotten children

Frances Emerson's truism that "what matters is the love, nourishment, protection and opportunity which a family can provide and which is every child's right" (Letters, 24/12) should include "in their country of origin".

The reasons for so many children residing in orphanages overseas are complex and will not be solved by families in other countries selectively adopting them. As I have seen working for many years in the Intercountry Adoption program, most prospective parents seek the youngest, healthiest children who have the least negative family background factors – not the most disadvantaged children.

Advocacy for intercountry adoption by celebrities who adopted children when living away from Australia is misleading. In reality, they are advocating avoidance of the legal requirements of *The Hague Convention on Protection of Children and Co-operation in Respect of Intercountry Adoption (1993)* designed to ensure that the most disadvantaged and vulnerable children are matched with the most suitable adoptive parents.

Penny Mackieson, social worker, Kew

Two days later, *The Age* published an excellent letter from the Manager of VANISH recommending careful review before any radical policy changes in relation to intercountry adoption were made. However, in another letter from a "senior counsel," I was accused of having provided an "inaccurate legal opinion," and criticised for "needlessly causing heartache to many couples seeking to adopt" and for being an "idealistically driven social worker."

On 25 January 2014, *The Age* reported that a campaign group was calling for action in regard to the adoptions by Australians of several children from India that were subsequently found to be illegal. I responded with a letter, which was published two days later.

Published in *The Age*, Monday, 27 January 2014

Safeguards at risk

Rory Callinan's article ("Campaign group calls for action on 'illegal' adoption of Indian children", 25/1) highlights the very reason for establishment and proper implementation of the Hague Convention on Protection of Children and Co-operation in Respect of Inter-country Adoption (1993), which sets out safeguards to ensure inter-country adoption takes place in the best interests of the child.

Australia is a signatory to, and has ratified, this convention. It is the ratification part – involving reviewing and improving the safeguards in place – on which the Indian authorities have been working hard since 2010.

Inter-country adoption advocates complain about the amount of red tape and length of time it takes to adopt a child from overseas. However, the processes involved and time required to undertake them are crucial to ensuring that a child is genuinely in need of inter-country adoption and subsequently matched to the most suitable adoptive parents.

Prime Minister Tony Abbott wishes to change the adoption system in Australia to make it easier and faster for prospective parents to adopt children from overseas. I do not see how this can be achieved without compromising the safeguards, particularly, for the children involved. Act in haste, repent at leisure, Mr Abbott.

Penny Mackieson, Kew

The stories relating to intercountry adoption continued. On 9 February, the *Sunday Age* reported that a Victorian man's contributions to an orphanage in Ethiopia were helping to build better lives for children affected by AIDS through provision of an intensive program designed to find and support a suitable alternative family for each child within their extended family network in their country of origin. My letter to the *Sunday Age* was published in the next edition.

Published in *Sunday Age*, Sunday, 16 February 2014

A humanitarian model

Geoff Hucker's contributions to helping build better lives for children affected by AIDS, one at a time, in an orphanage in Ethiopia ("Orphans find their champion as Torquay pilot fulfils a dream in Ethiopia", 9/2) are outstanding. His work is similar to that in Cambodia of Jenny McAuley and her family, about which Martin Flanagan wrote ("Beating true for the red and blue", *The Age*, 9/6/12).

These humanitarian models should be championed. They provide ethical, intensively supported pathways for children to find a suitable alternative family in their extended family network, or a foster family, and a positive future – in their countries of origin. It is a great shame that Deborra-Lee Furness and her high-profile, wealthy friends do not see fit to throw their considerable support behind this type of work. Instead, Ms Furness prefers to champion the "rescue" model whereby one child at a time is removed, potentially from their extended family, as well as from their country, culture and language – via inter-country adoption.

It's not too late for Prime Minister Abbott. There's still time for him to learn about the lifelong negative repercussions of intercountry adoption for the children concerned and their families and countries of origin, and about better and less expensive models that can and should be pursued in their countries of origin to assist these most vulnerable children.

Penny Mackieson, Kew

This letter generated deep resentment from another letter writer who accused me of having "negatively juxtaposed Geoff Hucker's work" with people like him and his wife, who were adoptive parents to two children from overseas. He took exception to my "idealism" – an often-used reversal to put me down when, in fact, it is prospective and adoptive parents who are frequently overly idealistic about what would be achieved by them adopting a child from overseas. The letter writer was also derogatory about my place of residence – "middle-class Kew." This seemed to me rather too personal, even if it was irrelevant.

My letter writing campaign ramped up to such an extent that by the end of February 2014 I was emailing *The Age*'s letters editor on the subject of adoption at least weekly, depending on how annoyed I had become on reading each day's newspaper. I realised I was probably sending so many letters that the editors figured me a nuisance. Still, I was not fazed. I *needed* to write those letters; it was the editors' choice whether or not to publish any of them. I also tried my hand with further opinion pieces, but to no avail.

On 19 March 2014, three letters were published in *The Age* regarding Australian billionaire Andrew Forrest's 'noble' fight against global slavery and human trafficking. My response to the newspaper pointed out that poverty exists because capitalism inherently favours accumulation of wealth by a few, and slavery exists because capitalism creates market conditions conducive to it. Slavery and human trafficking exploit people living in poverty – just as the practice of intercountry adoption exploits young women and children living in poverty, and encourages illegal practices for financial gain in the procurement of children to meet the demands of the adoption market created by wealthy westerners. My letter was not published.

On the evening of 25 March 2014, I watched a television report on *SBS Dateline* about the thriving 'voluntourism' industry capitalising on westerners wanting to give time and money to assist 'orphans' in Nepal, where shonky orphanage operators seduce poverty-stricken families into handing over their children promising a better life and education, but use the children to attract thousands of dollars for themselves.

The same day I made efforts with a couple of newspapers to debunk the myth spread by Ms Furness that the state government program providers were responsible for the delays in the intercountry adoption process. In addition, Mr Abbott's plan to expand the number of partner countries was unlikely to achieve any real change in the domestic intercountry adoption programs due to the significant mismatch between the needs of the children identified by the countries of origin as requiring overseas adoption (older/special needs children) and the characteristics of children Australians wish to adopt (healthy infants). His plan was, however, likely to fuel the illicit baby trafficking market overseas. Publication success evaded me on these matters.

In April, an article in *The Age* questioned why the Australian Government had refused to commit to the new system enabling children to raise complaints of human rights violations to the United Nations. I emailed in reply, asserting that the government was undoubtedly reluctant to expose itself to international scrutiny of its child welfare policies. This was because it knew it would be shamed for the heavy handed nature of its treatment of families of asylum seeker children and communities of Indigenous Australian children. Further, it would draw criticism for its preference to invest in expensive middle-class family formation services that exploit vulnerable children and their most often poor families: for example, through its plans to expand and expedite the adoption of overseas and local children. The government would not be praised for its failure to prioritise spending on basic welfare programs for the people who needed them most. Sadly, my letter was not published.

It was becoming increasingly evident to me that the task of persuading mainstream print media – including a generally centrist newspaper like *The* Age – to view adoption practices from a perspective other than the would-be parents' was very difficult, if not impossible. It seemed like there was an unspoken, yet pervasive, agenda regarding these issues. I felt that not only did the editors agree with the pro-adoption lobbyists, they also had a stake in ensuring those views dominated the stories they published and thus set the parameters for the public discourse. I concluded that if *The Age* would not publish the opinion pieces I occasionally submitted, then I would simply have to maintain my flow of letters.

On 3 May 2014, *The Age* reported on the COAG meeting held the previous day: "In an unusually light agenda ... ministers agreed to move forward on a plan to provide a new national intercountry adoption service for all Australians wanting to adopt a child overseas." It was also reported that "the federal government is spending nearly $20 million to push its hardline message of deterrence to asylum seekers, telling people from some of the poorest and most desperate countries not to come to Australia." My email pointed out the irony of these reports. The reader was asked to imagine explaining to an intercountry adopted child that, although Australia refused to assist vulnerable people seeking asylum from Afghanistan, Bangladesh, Burma, India, Indonesia, Iraq, Lebanon, Malaysia, Pakistan, Somalia, Sri Lanka, Sudan, Thailand and Vietnam to settle here, an exception was made for them because of their adoptive parents' desperation to provide a loving home to an overseas 'orphan'. My letter was not published.

On 5 May 2014, Mr Abbott released a statement saying, "The Commonwealth Government is committed to adoption reform ... to help more Australian families to adopt." The same day the *Herald Sun* newspaper reported that "Prime Minister Tony Abbott said the [new] federal agency will make it cheaper and easier for Australian families hoping to adopt children from overseas ... Adoption campaigner Deborra-lee Furness ... said she hoped programs would be established with other countries such as Cambodia and Vietnam." Presumably, this would be via bilateral arrangements, as neither country was in a position to fully implement the requirements of the *Hague Convention.* Once again, my letter to *The Age* on this matter was not published; nor was my similarly angry letter on the same topic sent the following day.

On 10 May 2014, *The Age* published an editorial opinion ("Political reform would promote fiscal reform") which asserted that "middle-class and corporate welfare should be cut." This seemed inconsistent with its editorial opinion of 23 December 2013 in which it applauded Prime Minister Abbott's decision to make it easier and faster for Australians to adopt children from overseas. Intercountry adoption was always intended as a last resort welfare program for children with additional special needs from less affluent countries, not a first resort financially-assisted family formation service for well-off Australians. Mr Abbott should know from the recent *Report of the Interdepartmental Committee on Intercountry Adoption* (April 2014) that:

- "there are misconceptions about intercountry adoption;"
- "a majority of the overall processing time takes place overseas ... rather than Australian processes;"
- "it is not possible to substantially impact the rate of adoption [due to factors] beyond Australia's control;"
- "each intercountry adoption application is increasingly resource intensive with the forecasted 2012–2013 national average cost for government per adoption estimated at approximately $50,000;" and
- "the highly specialised [nature of the program falls outside the Commonwealth government's expertise and] applies equally to domestic adoption and childcare arrangements."

And yet, the Prime Minister apparently planned to radically change delivery arrangements for intercountry adoption by centralising the program under the Commonwealth government. In the process he would be expending substantially more taxpayer funds in order to "improve the experience of prospective adoptive parents." My letter was not published.

On 11 May 2014, the *Sunday Age* published an editorial opinion ("Stolen children, stolen future") rightly asserting that "we should all with one voice" speak up for the 300 or so girls abducted in Nigeria by fanatical Islamist group, Boko Haram. I agreed that the unimpressive nature of the world's reaction during the first few weeks of this terrible incident "was less than impressive." However, it was only to be expected given the hypocrisy inherent in condemning the stealing of children from poverty-stricken communities in developing countries when, simultaneously, wealthy westerners benefit from similar activities conducted by child trafficking rings seeking to profit from the demands of the intercountry adoption market. My letter was not published.

The same day, a heart-warming article about an Australian couple's adoption of two children from Cambodia – outside Australia's domestically delivered intercountry adoption programs – appeared in *Sunday Life* (*Sunday Age*). I emailed a letter noting there was a complete failure to mention the lifelong complexities and challenges of overseas adoption. The joy of becoming adoptive parents is tempered with the significant losses experienced by the children – of their name, family, culture, language and country of origin – which will challenge their identity and sense of belonging throughout their lives. I expressed hope that the parents had received comprehensive preparation through a *Hague Convention* compliant agency and that they were linked in with appropriate post-adoption supports. My letter was not published.

On 13 May 2014, the Abbott government delivered its first federal budget, savagely slashing billions of dollars of funding from welfare programs, education, health services and foreign aid aimed at fighting poverty. I wrote to *The Age* the next day addressing the uncivilised nature of this budget. I focussed particularly on the hypocrisy of Federal Treasurer Joe Hockey's line that "the states run schools; the states run hospitals" and that the states should, therefore, take responsibility for funding them, given that the states also run child protection and out-of-home care (including local and intercountry adoption), yet the Prime Minister had decided that the federal government would now run intercountry adoption. Making the intercountry adoption program into a Rolls Royce family formation service for well-off Australians contradicted the government's policy for "people to move from a culture of entitlement to a culture of opportunity." I did not expect my letter to be printed – and it was not!

On 15 May 2014, an article in *The Age* questioned how the Australian Government could consider sending refugees to Cambodia when that country refused to help more than 20,000 of its own people who were displaced by a rail project designed to fight poverty. I similarly questioned how the Australian Government could consider establishing an intercountry adoption program with the same country when it knew that despite a reportedly large number of children in institutional care there, most of them had parents or relatives and were placed in orphanages due to poverty. Historically, there have been concerns about child trafficking and corruption in Cambodia and significant resources would be required to correctly identify children and investigate their backgrounds to ensure eligibility for intercountry adoption. I was outraged that the Abbott government was prepared to trade desperate people seeking asylum in Australia for children from poverty-stricken families in Cambodia. My letter was not published; nor was a similar one that I emailed later.

On 19 May 2014, *The Age* published another editorial regarding the abduction of the schoolgirls in Nigeria. I noted with disappointment that the newspaper did not editorialise in March when it reported the rescue of 382 babies abducted for 'adoption' and the arrest of 1094 suspects by police in Beijing, China, in an operation to close down internet-based baby trafficking rings. Nor did it acknowledge the first anniversary of the national bi-partisan apology to those affected by past policies and practices of adoption in Australia. I questioned *The Age* on its apparent absence of moral outrage regarding the unethical 'fake orphan' and often-illegal child removal practices in poverty-stricken communities overseas to meet the demands of the 'baby market' created by wealthy westerners, including Australians. I correctly predicted that my letter would not be published.

May 25 was International Missing Children's Day, though there was no mention of it in the *Sunday Age* that day. I wrote two letters to *The Age* about it, one before and one after, noting the similarity of the severe emotional trauma and lifelong psychological damage that can impact internationally abducted children and their families left behind with that affecting intercountry adopted children and their families of origin. Neither letter was published.

On 31 May 2014, a feature article in *Good Weekend* (*The Age*) provided an edited extract from *Run for Your Life*, Jill Jolliffe's recently published book about her adoption and reunion story. I emailed a letter about the story, which was published on 14 June 2014 under the title "Finding my birth mother" but significantly edited. Here is the original text:

Saturday, 31 May 2014

> Many thanks to you and Jill Jolliffe for sharing Jill's remarkable adoption and reunion story (May 31). Emotionally and physically abused by her adoptive mother and stepfather, Jill has been brave and resilient in dealing with the negative lifelong impacts of her traumatic childhood. Jill rightfully stated that her adoptive parents "were unsuitable to adopt children" and questioned what, if any, assessment of them had been conducted by the relevant authorities.
>
> Screening, assessment and preparation procedures for prospective adoptive parents have come a long way since Jill's adoption, reflected in Australia's ratification in 1998 of the *Hague Convention on Protection of Children and Cooperation in Respect of Intercountry Adoption*, which sets out the ethical principles and legal requirements ('red tape') to ensure adoption takes place in the best interests of the child in both the receiving and origin countries.
>
> However, these important safeguards are at serious risk of being eroded through the Commonwealth government's move

> to take over delivery of intercountry adoption, given the Prime Minister has fully embraced celebrity pro-adoption advocate Deborra-lee Furness's campaign (National Adoption Awareness Week) to make it much easier, faster and cheaper for Australians to adopt children.[24]

On 1 June 2014, an article in the *Sunday Age* related the story of an Australian child who was the victim of parental child trafficking by her father and his Egyptian family. There was still no mention of International Missing Children's Day. I duly reiterated the messages of my previous letters. Legal decisions associated with such cases often result in custodial arrangements which cause loss of the child's access to, and connection with, half their family as well as their language, culture, name and nationality of origin. Such decisions violate the child's rights and can cause severe emotional trauma and lifelong psychological damage to both the child and their family. These are the same impacts as those associated with intercountry adoption, though the latter children lose access to, and connection with, *all* members of their family of origin. I had no success in regard to publication.

The next day, I questioned how much additional money Australia would give to Cambodia in exchange for legally stealing its children for adoption. I knew that adoption campaigner Deborra-lee Furness had previously recommended "re-routing the funds from foreign aid" to fund "tax benefits to families who adopt from overseas,"[25] so I suggested that it must be an enticing amount, indeed. My letter was not published.

Later that day I sent a long email to both *The Age* and the *Herald Sun* after learning that the Australian Government was endeavouring to speed legislative amendments through

24 The edits in the published version include that: "Thankfully" was inserted before "screening"; "assessment" was deleted from between "screening" and "preparation"; "Jill's adoption" was replaced with "Jolliffe's time"; and everything after "Jolliffe's time" was deleted.

25 See Jackman (2011, p. 43).

parliament for the granting of Australian citizenship. This would make it much easier for expatriate Australians to adopt children in countries not party to the *Hague Convention*. My worst fears about Tony Abbott's 'reform' of intercountry adoption were being realised, as encapsulated in my first letter published in *The Age* on 26 December 2013. Outraged, I noted Mr Abbott was well aware that adoptions by expatriate Australians were not subject to the same high standard of screening, preparation and assessment required under the *Hague Convention* as were adoptions arranged in Australia. Expatriate families were not linked in with appropriate support systems when they returned to Australia with their adopted children. I reiterated my warning that Mr Abbott's 'reform' of intercountry adoption would fuel the fake orphan and child trafficking activities of unscrupulous people in developing countries, and would lead to a significant increase in adoption breakdowns in Australia. I received no responses to my letters.

On 24 June 2014, I attended a session convened by *The Age* on how to write comment and letters that get published. What I had for some months suspected was confirmed – that I was probably clogging up the Inbox of the letters editor, Elizabeth Minter, with my frequent emails. Ms Minter was far too polite to mention my name specifically, though I felt the word 'pest' was never far from her thoughts. Still, I was able to have a quick chat at the end of the session with the editorial writer, Leonie Wood, regarding what I perceived as *The Age*'s inconsistency in campaigning for the rights of asylum seekers and their children from desperately poor and politically volatile countries, but not for the rights of children in 'orphanages' and their families living in desperate poverty in developing countries in the context of intercountry adoption. Ms Wood kindly suggested that I send her some background information, which I did, also apologising to Ms Minter and promising that I would bombard her Inbox less often. Little did I realise how difficult a promise that would be to keep!

My habit of reading *The Age* from cover to cover over breakfast and composing and emailing a letter over my first coffee was well ingrained. However, I did endeavour to read and respond more regularly to other media outlets.

On 27 June 2014, I emailed a letter to *The Guardian* regarding the Australian Government's wilful and systematic abuse of human rights in implementing its asylum seeker policy. I highlighted the hypocrisy associated with its expenditure of millions to prevent desperate families from war-torn countries seeking refuge and resettlement in Australia and the considerable funds it would need to spend to implement measures to make it easier, faster and cheaper for Australian couples desperate to adopt children from developing countries. I criticised Australia's retrograde neo-liberal government for having no compunction in commodifying children and denying human rights to the world's most vulnerable people. My letter was not published.

On 21 July 2014, an emotive article recommending adoption of overseas HIV orphans appeared in *The Age*, coinciding with Melbourne's hosting of the Twentieth International AIDS Conference. Furious, I expressed my alarm to *The Age*, pointing out that it was vital to thoroughly assess people's motivations to adopt any intercountry child because the child comes traumatised from having lost their family, name, language, culture and country. This is in addition to any medical condition. Simply wanting to adopt an HIV-positive child from overseas did not mean a person was suitable to parent such a child. Australians adopted few overseas children with special needs for the same reason they adopted few such children domestically – most prospective adoptive parents seek healthy infants. The *Report of the Interdepartmental Committee on Intercountry Adoption* (April 2014) clearly debunked negative myths that the situation with intercountry adoption in Australia was due to "poor bureaucracy." It was institutionalised child abuse to not encourage and support education and development of suitable care options for HIV-children in their countries of origin, especially as there were many successful models. My letter was not published.

I was not the only one saying these things. On 8 September, an online article appeared in *The Conversation*, entitled "Australia puts children at risk by 'freeing up' the adoption market" by Patricia Fronek, Denise Cuthbert and Mary Keyes (Fronek, Cuthbert and Keyes, 2014), which reinforced my own position.

On 11 October 2014, I found buried in *The Age*, in an article by Mark Kenny entitled "Indigenous referendum date close," his report from the COAG meeting of the previous day noting that of the few concrete decisions, one was a commitment from the Commonwealth government to establish a single federal agency

> to steer hopeful parents of adopted children through Commonwealth agencies. "At the moment, if you want to adopt, you typically go to a state adoption agency, you consider the issue generally and at some point, often enough, you will decide that you are going to have a go at overseas adoption because that is more prospective than local adoption," Mr Abbott said. "Then, as things stand, you have got to navigate largely unaided a thicket of Commonwealth agencies."

I was struck by so many things at once that I barely knew where to begin. Firstly, that the article was purely from the perspective of the impatient adoptive/would-be adoptive parents. In fact, it sounded very much to me like something Ms Furness would say. Secondly, what Mr Abbott was quoted as having said sounded confused and was inaccurate. In my experience at ICAS, program staff assisted applicants every step of the way – with written instructions, face-to-face meetings, emails and frequent phone calls – through the plethora of documents required by both the overseas and Australian authorities, including the visa application process. Or was Mr Abbott, in fact, referring to prospective adoptive parents who decided to take matters into their own hands and head overseas for the purposes of adopting children as expatriate Australians? Certainly, at ICAS the staff were not permitted to advise on, or facilitate, the undertaking of such practices. I did not even bother writing to *The Age*. That day I truly felt I had failed in my endeavour to influence that newspaper into taking an interest in comprehensive reporting on issues associated with adoption.

But I did not give up writing altogether and, in November, this letter was published:

Published in *The Age*, Monday, 17 November 2014

Sucked in by celebrity

Simon Castles writes: "In the years after the triumph of Band Aid, charity and activism became less and less about grassroots action, and more and more about celebrity-driven spectacle." Sadly, this observation still – or is it again? – holds true in Australia. For example, Deborra-Lee Furness won NSW 2015 Australian of the Year for a misguided but popular campaign to "reform" inter-country adoption by making it easier, faster and cheaper for Australians to adopt children from Third World countries. The fact that the children's best interests would be best served if they were supported in extended/alternative families in their communities and countries of origin has been lost in the sycophantic hype associated with the celebrity.

Penny Mackieson, Kew

I had further success a few months later:

Published in *Sunday Age*, Sunday, 15 March 2015

Adoption a last resort

Since the 1980s, adoption has been rightly practised in Australia as a last resort alternative placement program for vulnerable children unable to live safely with their families, *not* as a family formation service for celebrities and the middle-class ("Blanchett baby put spotlight on adoption", 8/3).

Adoption violates numerous universal children's rights: it severs the legal, and often social and cultural, connections with family; and destroys the child's identity. The horrific legacy of the Stolen

Generations and the forced adoptions of previous decades has not stopped with the apologies; Tony Abbott is transforming intercountry adoption into a deregulated baby market.

Ever wondered why adoptees don't spruik for easier, faster and cheaper access to adoption? It's because they've experienced the traumatic losses and legacies inherent in adoption. Prospective adopters lobby because they have a misguided sense of entitlement. Adoption, like donor IVF and surrogacy, commodifies children.

Penny Mackieson, Kew

5.1.2 Local adoption

As mentioned earlier, I anticipated there would likely be moves for the states and territories – particularly those with Liberal-National Coalition governments – to embrace Prime Minister Tony Abbott's retrograde neo-liberal policy on intercountry adoption in local adoption policy, similar to the changes that were occurring in NSW. I thus anticipated that I would need to address local adoption policy developments as well. I did not have to wait long.

On 12 February 2014, an article appeared in *The Age* regarding the crisis in Australia whereby thousands of vulnerable children were residing in temporary out-of-home care placements. The solution recommended by The Centre for Independent Studies – a privately funded think-tank which supports free enterprise – was early adoption of the children. In responding, I pointed out that the article lacked analysis of the reasons for the significant increase in children entering the out-of-home care system and the over-representation of Aboriginal children. Further, Berry Street – a highly respected not-for-profit non-government agency with a long history supporting children and families in Victoria – recommended professionalising foster care as a solution. Early consideration of adoption from out-of-home care was tantamount to forced adoption practice and risked creating a new stolen generation. That this particular letter was not published was no real surprise. However, I began to wonder whether my emails might be touching a raw nerve with *The Age*. Was I identifying concerns and drawing parallels – expressing 'dangerous ideas' – about which that newspaper was uncomfortable?

On 17 May 2014, an article in *Good Weekend* told the positive reunion story of a locally adopted person with members of their family of origin. The next day I sent a letter, which was subsequently published.

Published in *Good Weekend*, *The Age*, Saturday, 31 May 2014

FAMILY REUNION

As an adoptee myself and a former senior social worker with Victoria's intercountry adoption program, I know that adoption and reunion stories are usually much more complex than those that are presented in the media, and can also be tempered with some lifelong negative challenges (May 17). Those affected by pre-1980s adoption policies deserve the full gamut of adoption stories to be told.

Penny Mackieson, Kew, VIC

In August 2014, this issue gained momentum as the Napthine government moved to place vulnerable children in adoption/permanent care after 12 months in circumstances where their families were unable to overcome child abuse or neglect concerns. The major risk with the government misguidedly reverting to a system of forced adoption was repeating the damaging mistakes of Australia's past. A pro-adoption system embraced prospective parents, while a pro-child system embraced permanency planning for vulnerable children. I wrote to *The Age* but my letter was not published.

On 26 August 2014, I sent a letter to *The Daily Telegraph* regarding an article about the glossy re-launch of Ms Furness's campaign organisation, National Adoption Awareness Week, to Adopt Change. I noted there were so many misleading statements about the adoption system in Australia that another article was needed, which I would be pleased to write. I argued that Ms Furness's pro-adoption agenda was misguided, and prioritised the desires and wishes of prospective adoptive parents over the rights of children to be supported and connected with their families and, for some, also their cultures. The evident embrace of Ms Furness's campaign by the current Commonwealth, NSW and Victorian governments was repeating the mistakes of Australia's past, whereby institutionalised policies and practices forced separation of children from their families to meet the supply of children demanded by middle-class infertile Australians seeking to form their families by adoption. I knew even before pressing the 'send' button that this letter would never be published.

On 28 August 2014, I emailed the *Herald Sun*, also regarding the re-launch of lobbyist organisation, Adopt Change. I noted that neither Ms Furness nor her new celebrity ambassadors had any qualifications or expertise in the welfare profession, let alone in adoption. Further, Ms Furness resided in the USA, yet was such a darling of the mainstream media in Australia that journalists failed to challenge the appropriateness of her pro-adoption campaign here. Finally, Ms Furness's so-called 'adoption reform work' made a mockery of the national bi-partisan apology made in March 2013 by then Labor Prime Minister Julia Gillard and Opposition Leader Tony Abbott to the thousands of Australians who have suffered from past policies and practices of adoption. Of course, this letter was not published either.

In September, the *Children, Youth and Families Amendment (Permanent Care and Other Matters) Bill 2014* was passed by the Victorian government. This legislation enshrines expeditious consideration of adoption for children entering out-of-home care through the child protection system, as does the similar piece of legislation passed in NSW in March 2014. The Victorian government did not seek feedback from key adoption stakeholder groups – such as VANISH, ARMS and Origins, and there was no open public consultation process on the legislation before its proposal to parliament. If not for the efforts of Labor MP Jenny Mikakos, then Shadow Minister for Community Services and Shadow Minister for Children, those stakeholder groups would probably not have even heard about the aspects of the legislation pertaining to adoption until it was passed. The legislation was slipped through parliament without fanfare; without proper reporting or questioning from the mainstream media. Public discussion was effectively stifled, including any opportunity to challenge the apparent resumption of 'forced adoption' policies and practices in Victoria.

On 22 October 2014, a report in *The Sydney Morning Herald* announced the finalists for the NSW 2015 Australian of the Year awards. Among them was Ms Furness who was incomprehensibly described as a "child advocate and adoption campaigner" – an oxymoron from my social work perspective. It was appalling to me that the general public did not understand someone who was an 'adoption campaigner' could not also claim to advocate for children – the two agendas were almost mutually exclusive. Someone who genuinely advocated for children would never advocate for adoption as the alternative care option of first choice, given that adoption terminates the child's legal and, often also, social relationships with their family of origin. Surely anyone could see that a Permanent Care Order was a significantly better option for the child?

Ms Furness was announced as the winner of the NSW 2015 Australian of the Year award on 10 November 2014 – the first weekday of Adopt Change's National Adoption Awareness Week, now morphed into a month-long event. Further insult was added to injury when, on 18 November, the *Family Confidential* program featuring Deborra-lee Furness and Hugh Jackman first televised on 4 February was replayed by *ABC1*. It seemed to me that this country's history of poor adoption policies and practices, which led to the national apology in March 2013, had already been forgotten. My guts churned with anxiety from then until the announcement would be made on 26 January 2015 that the 2015 Australian of the Year would also be awarded to Ms Furness. I was enormously relieved when it was awarded to Rosie Batty, the courageous Victorian campaigner against domestic violence whose son Luke was murdered by his father in early 2014.

Also in November 2014, with a state election imminent, an article appeared in *The Age* entitled 'Rainbow parents call for adoption rights' bemoaning that LGBTI (lesbian, gay, bi-sexual, transgender and intersex) people in Victoria were not permitted to adopt their foster children, even after having become their permanent carers. The reporter had failed to understand that adoption by anyone, regardless of sexual orientation, was not necessary and, indeed, was not appropriate once a Permanent Care Order had been issued. A *Permanent Care* Order was exactly that – a legal order determining the child's caregiving guardians until the child attained 18 years of age. Further, because adoption was seldom found to be in the best interests of a child, an adoption order was rarely issued.

I was annoyed with the general lack of understanding in the media and community about adoption and, in particular, with the inappropriateness of Rainbow Families apparently trying to hijack adoption and turn it into an election issue for their own purposes. Surely the real issue was whether adoption should continue to be available at all, given it violated the rights of vulnerable children. Why were people so obsessed with legal ownership of children – as if they were chattels? The key thing for children was the nature of the relationships established and maintained with them by significant adults, rather than the name of the legal order which enabled or supported this to happen. However, I managed to refrain from emailing a letter to *The Age* about it; perhaps satisfied with publication of my letter the same day about the late Gough Whitlam ... or perhaps unwilling to risk being accused of political incorrectness, even though unfounded.

Finally, again that November, as if in response to my plea, *Sunday Life* ran an article about the reunions of three women and their mothers who had been separated by adoption. In fact, in response to a request for potential interviewees directed to VANISH, I had spoken via phone beforehand with the freelance journalist who wrote the article. As it turned out, the editor was not nearly as keen for me to be interviewed as the journalist was to interview me. Still, I considered it important to encourage publication by *The Age* of perspectives other than adoptive parents and prospective adoptive parents and so submitted my feedback, which was subsequently printed.

Published in *Sunday Life*, *Sunday Age*, Sunday, 7 December 2014

TIES THAT BIND

Many thanks to the three women adoptees who shared with Michaela Fox their personal stories of reunion with their mothers ("First Contact", November 23). Such a small sample can only touch on some of the complexities of adoption but this article was a welcome change from all the stories narrowly focused on the immediate joys for adoptive parents.

Penny Mackieson, Kew, Vic

Also on 7 December, another article appeared in *The Age* on 'adoption rights' for gay couples. Given that the new Andrews Labor government, elected at the end of November 2014, had so recently campaigned on implementing gay rights, I felt obliged to send a letter in response, despite my fear of it being misconstrued as anti-gay. My letter was published the following week with three sentences deleted, as follows:

Published in *Sunday Age*, *The Age*, Sunday, 14 December 2014

Children not a 'right'

"Gay couples to get adoption rights" (7/12) reflects the misguided purpose of adoption – to meet the "needs" of prospective adoptive parents by legally erasing the child's past. Even "open" adoption undermines the rights and best interests of children. Adoption severs the child's legal relationships with their parents, and enables the adoptive parents to also sever the social relationships – negatively and permanently affecting the child's identity development. In Victoria, permanent care is a preferable legal order to adoption for children – it legally secures a suitable alternative family, while preserving the child's identity and links with their parents. No adult has a "right" to adopt a child. Children are not chattels to be: owned; procured; used to legitimise ethically dubious third-party reproductive methods; or commodified in the political ideologies and struggles of adults. Martin Foley, the new Equality Minister, has an important role in implementing LGBTI rights, but this should not be done in isolation from other ministries or from consideration of the rights of children.

Penny Mackieson, Kew

The deleted sentences were: "Children are the most vulnerable in our community and should have their own advocates. The Abbott government has rushed headlong into repeating the mistakes of Australia's past unethical adoption practices by embracing the pro-adoption agenda. *There should be no changes to the Victorian Adoption Act without a full and comprehensive review* – as discussed by Jenny Mikakos, the new Minister for Families and Children, when Shadow Minister."

The rights of LGBTI people, particularly the issue of legalising same-sex marriages, continued to generate considerable discussion in the Australian media in 2015. My response to one of many opinion pieces in *The Age* on the topic was published in June.

Published in *The Age*, Friday, 12 June 2015

Children's needs extend beyond love

Steve Dow rightly argues that having children is not a prerequisite for heterosexual couples to marry, so should not be for homosexual couples ("Faith, bigotry and the children of gay parents", Comment, 10/6). However, I disagree that what matters most for the children of gay couples is having parents who love them. Love is not enough, although it has long been used as an excuse to commodify children and separate them from their biological parents. Yes, we should eliminate discrimination from the marriage statutes and legalise same-sex unions. But no, we should not link this argument to the best interests of children. No adult – heterosexual or homosexual – has the right to a child. However, children have universal rights – including to be raised by and/or have ongoing relationships with the mother and father who created them, whether married or not.

Penny Mackieson, Kew

5.1.3 Surrogacy

Another topic included in my letter writing campaign was surrogacy which featured prominently in the news throughout 2014. I see strong parallels between surrogacy and adoption – both for the children who have no choice in the matter but must live with the negative consequences of their parents' decisions for their entire lives; and for the young women who bear the children who may be persuaded or pressured into doing so, believing they are giving the ultimate altruistic gift of life to deserving others, but may well come to regret their personal decision for the rest of their lives. The commodification of babies is a feature shared by adoption and surrogacy; and the exploitation of young women's reproductive capacity – as egg providers and 'baby carriers' – is a feature of surrogacy practices, just as the exploitation of young women living with poverty and disadvantage is a feature of adoption practices. As both surrogacy and adoption violate children's rights and exploit young women, discussion of one seems to me incomplete without mention of the other – particularly given my direct knowledge that many ICAS applicants also pursued overseas commercial surrogacy in order to ensure they would not miss out on obtaining a child.

In February 2014, there were two feature articles on surrogacy in the *Sunday Age*. One reported on the damaging psychological effects on mothers who give birth through overseas commercial surrogacy. Another reported one woman's offence at the suggestion that mothers who give birth to children via commercial surrogacy will suffer the same negative effects from separation trauma after birth and subsequent exclusion from the children's lives as do mothers separated from their babies via adoption. My unpublished arguments in response to these reports included that the young women financially exploited through surrogacy comprise the same group exploited through past policies and practices of forced adoption. Further, surrogacy means that a child could potentially have three mothers (a genetic mother aka egg provider, a birth mother, and a socio-legal mother), each important to the child's history and future identity and well-being.

The issue gained further momentum in early August 2014 when the tragic story of Gammy, a Down syndrome baby born via commercial surrogacy in Thailand, broke. He was abandoned by his Australian commissioning parents in favour of his 'healthy' twin sister. I wrote a letter stating that commercial surrogacy inherently exploited young women living in poverty. Commercial surrogacy was illegal in Australia for this very reason, and altruistic surrogacy was rare due to the complexities and significant risks involved. Privately, I considered 'best practice' surrogacy was no surrogacy at all, just as 'best practice' adoption was no adoption at all. However, in the interests of improving my chances of publication, I stated in my letter that "best practice surrogacy is well-regulated altruistic surrogacy." My letter further argued that infertile Australians had no compunction about utilising unregulated overseas commercial markets like those in Thailand and India in order to obtain 'healthy' children. Sad stories like that of baby Gammy were truly appalling and likely to be more common than reported, given that mainstream Australian media empathised with prospective/commissioning parents and glamourised and popularised their success stories. Such stories led to condoning and encouraging overseas commercial surrogacy – just as it did overseas commercial donor IVF and intercountry adoption. The Australian Government was creating easier and cheaper pathways for expatriate Australians to adopt children overseas, now that the supply of 'healthy' infants through the regulated domestically provided intercountry adoption programs had dried up. When would Australians accept that having children – particularly, healthy children – was not an entitlement? When would Australians recognise that unregulated overseas practices exploit destitute young women and violate the human rights and future psychological and physical well-being of the children? When would Australians prioritise the rights of the children above their own wishes to form their families? My letter was not published but a later one was.

Published in *The Age*, Monday, 4 August 2014

> **Why commercial surrogacy is wrong**
>
> Yes, Tony Abbott, Gammy's story is "incredibly sad". But your comment about the pitfalls in the surrogacy "business" and your expectation that the government will make representations to Thai authorities on behalf of Australian couples reflect an appalling acceptance of the commodification of overseas children and a belief that the rights of prospective Australian parents are more important than those of overseas parents.
>
> I applaud the Australians who donated to fund Gammy's medical treatment. However, I condemn those who offered to adopt Gammy. He is deeply loved and is being appropriately cared for by his Thai family. Their primary problem is poverty. Their secondary problem was to have trusted well-off Westerners from a country where commercial surrogacy and forced/closed adoption are illegal for good reason.
>
> **Penny Mackieson, Kew**

By this time I had so many concerns about surrogacy and how the issue was being reported that I wrote more fully on the topic to *The Age*. Why, if Australian commissioning parents were so concerned about the medical and psychological welfare of their pregnant Thai surrogates, would they choose to engage in commercial surrogacy in the first place? If Australian commissioning parents were so concerned about 'humanitarian' factors, why would they deliberately choose to create children who would suffer lifelong negative psychological impacts, as would their surrogate mothers, from being separated at birth? How did the breakdown of one altruistic surrogacy arrangement in Australia become a good reason to commercialise surrogacy here? If Australian commissioning parents were prepared to take advantage of a friend with whom they had a positive prior social relationship, why would they be less likely to take advantage of a young, probably less educated or financially well-off, woman they would meet solely for the purposes of surrogacy and with whom they would have only a commercial relationship? And what about the child's right to have ongoing contact with each of his or her parents – caregiving, biological and genetic? How could the child's rights be protected through a commercial surrogacy contract which was primarily focused on the wishes of the commissioning parents?

Indeed, as stated in an article by Allison Pearson in the *Sunday Age* on 10 August, I agreed it was "obvious that the safeguards governing intercountry adoption need to be extended to cover surrogacy"[26] – despite the fact that the Abbott government was endeavouring to erode those safeguards by making it easier, faster and cheaper for Australians to adopt children from overseas. However, I disagreed that a fairy tale outcome for baby Gammy would be achieved by him being "offered for adoption" with his twin sister ("as a pigeon pair") by an Australian couple. The fairy tale outcome for Gammy would be for his twin sister to be returned to the care of his mother in Thailand, and for Australians to contribute sufficient funds to a trust to ensure she was supported to adequately provide for the raising of both children through to adulthood. I despaired that many Australians did not appear to appreciate the commercialisation of reproduction and commodification of children through surrogacy, donor IVF and intercountry adoption. All of these

26 See Pearson (2014).

practices are detrimental to the children's short- and long-term psychological welfare. The misguided obsession of the Australian media with highlighting the desperate plights of infertile people seeking to acquire babies and their subsequent joy on becoming parents masked an underbelly of opportunistic exploitation, albeit often unintended, by those prospective parents and the inherent lifelong, albeit often publicly invisible, trauma and psychological damage for the children. Western commercial opportunism could never justify humanitarian abomination and human rights violations. Unfortunately, my letter was not published.

Thick-skinned and undeterred, on 11 August 2014, I emailed *The Age* asserting that Australian laws did not 'force' prospective Australian parents to travel to Third World countries to obtain children – whether via commercial surrogacy, commercial anonymous donor IVF or expatriate intercountry adoption. These practices should all be banned because of the dubious ethics involved and the tendency for exploitation of people living in poverty. Some prospective Australian parents chose to engage in these practices; therefore, it was they who should feel ashamed and take responsibility for the outcomes when things went awry. Why, if all surrogate mothers engaged in commercial surrogacy for reasons of altruism, were there not more children born of altruistic surrogacy arrangements in Australia? Australia's domestic ban on commercial surrogacy had nothing to do with sexism – rather it was designed to protect the rights of women living in poverty and their children. I concluded that the real tragedy in the baby Gammy case was the desperation of prospective parents in seeking to have healthy babies and their inability to accept that having children was not their right. Again, my letter was not published.

The next day, *The Age* published an editorial on the topic of commercial surrogacy. In my response, I argued that the medical profession in this country clearly had a significant financial interest in growing its assisted reproductive industry.

Therefore, it could not be trusted to provide objective advice on such ethically complex and emotive issues any more than could desperate prospective parents. The medical profession had made a mess in regard to donor IVF laws, whereby a substantial group of people donor-conceived pre-1988 were unable to access records about their biological fathers because of a ludicrous promise made to them by well-meaning doctors that the personal details of the 'sperm donors' would forever remain undisclosed to any children born to them. This decision to deny the human rights of the children to information about, and contact with, their biological fathers was made despite extensive evidence available from adoption research at the time regarding the likely detrimental long-term impacts on the identity formation and psychological well-being of the children. I disagreed that "Australians generally accept surrogacy," given they do not even recognise the commonality of issues inherent in surrogacy, donor IVF and adoption, let alone understand those issues from the child's perspective. I asserted that Prime Minister Tony Abbott should have brought his concerns regarding intercountry adoption "into the open for this nation to have a comprehensive and properly informed debate about it"[27] *before* he announced his plans to 'reform' it. I expressed my grave concern that any national debate about commercial surrogacy would once again be dominated by the powerful and greedy elements in the medical profession in conjunction with desperate prospective parents. This would be promoted by populist mainstream media in isolation from the debates about anonymous donor IVF and intercountry adoption. Thus, Australia would rush headlong into repeating the mistakes of its past by creating, via ethically dubious practices, new generations of children who would suffer lifelong negative psychological consequences. I concluded that the best interests of children should be the paramount consideration. My letter was not published.

27 Quoted from *The Age's* editorial on commercial surrogacy, 12 August 2014.

I followed up with another letter in response to columnist Julie Szego's neo-liberal pro-commercial surrogacy views which normalised all practices engaged in by prospective western parents to obtain children. She denied that money provided the primary inducement for destitute women to engage in such practices and, thus, that such practices were exploitative. She ignored the children's perspective and the prospect of lifelong negative consequences. If Ms Szego had a social work background rather than a legal one, she might better understand the parallels between commercial surrogacy and intercountry adoption. In both, there are difficulties in ensuring that applicants had suitable motivations and expectations, even when the system was "tightly regulated and limited in scope,"[28] in which case applicants would complain about perceived excessive 'red tape' and seek deregulation. Legalising commercial surrogacy would consolidate Australia as a land of hypocrisy, rather than of maturity. My letter was not published. However, two excellent opinion pieces – one by Dr Sonia Allan ("Commercial surrogacy is not the way forward," published on 5 August 2014) and the other by Dr Renate Klein ("Wombs are not merely suitcases for babies," published on 20 August 2014) – were an antidote to the neo-liberal opinions. The latter article generated positive feedback from other letter writers and I was encouraged that there were others who shared a similar perspective to mine.

Still, *The Age*'s clear pro-adoption position and increasingly pro-donor IVF and pro-commercial surrogacy bias was a persistent source of frustration. I was unable to encourage the newspaper into a more comprehensive and integrated approach to reporting on these issues. So, on 22 August, I made another submission to *The Age* for an opinion piece entitled "No good reason to commercialise surrogacy," but was not successful.

That same month though, my pitch to the online *Overland* journal for an article with the working title, "Advocating for

28 See Szego (2014).

vulnerable children: The case against overseas adoption, commercial surrogacy and anonymous donor IVF," was successful. Published under the headline "The overseas adoption option" (Mackieson, 2014a), the article linked my concerns about the planned government changes to adoption with the tragic commercial surrogacy case of baby Gammy in Thailand. Many comments criticising my position – apparently from intercountry adoptive parents – flowed in over the following days, though ceased when another intercountry adoptive parent added a comment indicating agreement with my arguments. An intercountry adoptee later posted that she was "amazed at the responses ... Obviously hit a raw nerve!" She applauded me for giving my "professional opinion, knowing what kind of response it will draw from some," and stated her belief that "we need more open and critical discussions in our society on these issues." I was heartened that there were other people who felt the same way I did.

On 24 August 2014, I pitched an idea for a feature article to the National Bulletin of the AASW (Australian Association of Social Workers), of which I am a long-time member. In light of the controversy associated with the baby Gammy case and recent developments in both overseas and domestic adoption policy, I called for social work leadership in developing a strong pro-child approach in relation to the highly complex, sensitive and emotive social policy area of reproduction and family formation. My article, "Surrogacy and Adoption," was published in the Summer 2014 edition. I suggested that it was timely "for the AASW to take the lead – to consult widely with its members; to develop a position which links the many issues common to adoption, donor IVF and surrogacy; and to take a strongly pro-child social justice stance" (Mackieson, 2014b, pp. 15–16).

The momentum around the issue of surrogacy continued and, in September, another of my letters was printed.

Published in *The Age*, Wednesday, 3 September 2014

Kids aren't commodities

Were we appalled on hearing of another unregulated Thai commercial surrogacy case gone wrong in which the Australian biological/commissioning father allegedly sexually abused his twins aged under 10? We should be. Similarly, we should be concerned at the move under Tony Abbott's adoption reform to expand a deregulated pathway for Australians living overseas to adopt children, thereby avoiding the "red tape" associated with the best practice regulation of inter-country adoption domestically under a Hague Convention.

Many commentators are arguing for a global ban on commercial surrogacy. I agree. There should also be global bans on adoption outside the safeguards of the Hague Convention and on anonymous donor conception. Children are human beings and deserve much better than to be treated as just another commodity in an exploitative, globalised free market.

Penny Mackieson, Kew

I was inspired to persist when supportive comments from other letter writers followed in subsequent days.

Even the TV pages of *The Age* did not escape my attention. I was compelled to write to the *Green Guide* after the broadcast of an *SBS* episode of *Insight* which was shamelessly biased in favour of legalising commercial surrogacy. Swedish investigative journalist and author, Kajsa Ekis Ekman, was set up as the lone dissenting voice. The voices of children, now adults, born of surrogacy were notably absent. I argued that without more balanced reporting in the mainstream media, prospective Australian Prime Ministers might as well start writing their national apologies to the next traumatised generations now. While my letter was not printed, another was that expressed similar sentiments.

On 14 September 2014, an article appeared in *The Age* entitled "New Thai surrogacy concerns" by Lindsay Murdoch with AM Sandford. It stated: "individual cases continue to arise that highlight the morally fraught terrain of the surrogacy industry." This was the first article I had seen all year in *The Age* by a journalist that was not blatantly in favour of commercial surrogacy for Australians. While it was a welcome relief, I did not dare imagine that my letters were making a difference to what the editors chose to publish.

The surrogacy debate continued throughout September and I again managed to get a letter printed in *The Age*, this time in the weekend magazine supplement.

Published in *Good Weekend*, *The Age*, Saturday, 27 September 2014

ANOTHER WOMAN'S CHILD

Pro-surrogacy lobbyists are, evidently, just as misguided, relentless and favoured by the media as pro-adoption lobbyists (September 13). In your story we are presented with the contradictory rationalisations of three "altruistic" surrogate mothers – two appear addicted to pregnancy, and one is willing to risk her health and her own children's welfare to pursue another surrogate pregnancy. The lone voice of a child born via surrogacy was presented through the words of her biological aunt/surrogate mother. Why not report on the children's perspectives, independent of their biological and surrogate parents, via community-based support organisations such as VANISH?

Penny Mackieson, Kew, Vic

Even in November 2014, the Baby Gammy story was still making news. On 29 November, it was reported that "Thailand's military-dominated parliament has voted overwhelmingly to ban commercial surrogacy three months after Fairfax revealed the plight of baby Gammy." My immediate relief at this news was tempered by information from another source that the lucrative commercial surrogacy market in Thailand was already deep into the process of re-location to Nepal.

5.1.4 Sperm and egg donation

Sperm and egg donation is another aspect of the commercialisation of babies that has close parallels with the issues raised by adoption. The key issues for me are the deliberate violation of the child's rights to know identifying information about, have an ongoing relationship with and/or be raised by the mother or father who has 'donated' their egg or sperm for the child's creation; and that this is enabled through a dehumanising commercial contract without regard to the likely long-term negative consequences for the child, then adult's, identity development and health.

In March 2014, an article published in the *Sunday Age* discussed how single women were travelling to Greece for anonymous donor IVF treatment. My letter was published in the following edition.

Published in *Sunday Age*, Sunday, 30 March 2014

> **Protecting the children**
>
> There's another perspective to add to Alexandra Smith's thought-provoking article – that of the children born from anonymous donor embryos from overseas ("Women heading to Greece for IVF", 23/3).
>
> Aside from the potential impacts of any genetic physical and mental health issues, it can be anticipated that these children will have long-term identity development and psychological wellbeing challenges additional to those of most other children. As they mature they may struggle to understand how their mothers could have prioritised their "need" to have a child over their children's human right to know their biological history and to have the option of seeking contact with biological family members when they reach adulthood.
>
> Australia's laws aren't draconian but designed to protect the rights of the child. It's a shame these laws do not also prohibit Australians from shopping around overseas where the rights of children are not always as well protected and there are flourishing markets for babies and the means to produce them.
>
> **Penny Mackieson, Kew**

In April 2014, more articles appeared in the *Sunday Age* about single women pursuing parenthood via IVF with donor sperm and donor ova, fully aware their children may never have the opportunity to know the identity of their biological fathers, sometimes also their biological mothers, let alone have relationships with them. My primary concern with these stories was, again, that the perspective of the children was omitted and the lifelong negative consequences ignored. Seeing eggs and sperm reduced to the status of commodities was deeply discomforting to me. My letter on this topic was not selected for publication, but the issue continued to crop up in the newspapers throughout the remainder of the year.

A slightly different take on the use of sperm occurred in June 2014, when a report in the *Sunday Age* told the story of a woman who used the sperm of her deceased husband to have children. I wrote that children's rights were paramount, including their right to know both their parents. Lacking such opportunity could have profoundly negative long-term impacts on their psychological well-being. In my view, from an ethical standpoint it was not fair to conceive a child knowing she or he could never know their father – whether via IVF using the sperm of one's dead husband, or via anonymous donor IVF or surrogacy. My letter was not published, which led me to wonder whether questioning the 'right' to use a dead spouse's sperm was a no-go zone in the media.

In July, I sent a brief letter to the *Good Weekend* supplement of *The Age* expressing my hope that the story it ran that day about Sophia Turkiewicz resonated as deeply with people contemplating commercial anonymous donor IVF, surrogacy or adoption overseas as it did with me … "if your parent is abstract in your mind, there's always some missing thing you can never make whole". I shared, from my own experience as an adoptee, that I knew this unsettling feeling may plague the child lifelong. My letter was not published, but I dared to email another letter to the *Sunday Age* which was.

Published in *Sunday Age*, Sunday, 20 July 2014

Repeating mistakes

I'm relieved our laws prevent people from using an embryo containing DNA from more than two people, although disturbed that other countries are debating whether to allow the deceptively benign sounding "mitochondrial-replacement therapy" ("And baby makes 4", 13/7).

The drivers of the assisted reproductive industry are well-off infertile people who feel "entitled" to have a child and prioritise their desires over the significant risks/known negative impacts for any future person created who cannot consent to experimental procedures. Sadly, it is nothing new for morally questionable policies and practices involving children to be fuelled by the whims of wealthy Westerners – "assimilation" of indigenous children, criminalisation of asylum seekers, intercountry adoption, overseas commercial donor IVF and surrogacy and so on.

When will the West learn from the all-too-recent mistakes of its past? There are other, more ethical and beneficial ways of dealing with infertility, starting with grief and genetic counselling.

Penny Mackieson, Kew

In September 2014, I emailed my response to an article published in the *Sunday Age*, "Appeal to share the love." I argued that the capitalist commodification of babies was both shameless and relentless. Under the guise of a topical article, a free advertisement for Melbourne IVF – part of Virtus, one of Australia's biggest publicly-listed IVF companies – appeared on Father's Day, promoting sperm donation as a selfless act of altruism to assist infertile couples and spread the joy of becoming parents. Yet, donating sperm to an assisted reproductive business is not at all like donating blood to Red Cross. Blood is a potentially life-saving biological substance for the recipient, usually with no future ramifications for the donor. In recognising the best interests of donor-conceived children, ensuring their rights to know the identity of, and have contact with, their donor fathers, sperm donation is not – and should never have been – anonymous. A simple act of ejaculation into a beaker may be a gift from the perspective of the donor, the infertile parents and, especially, the IVF industry. But the perspective of a donor-conceived person could be compared with someone forcibly relinquished for adoption in an earlier era. Predictably, my letter was not published.

The same month, I also sent a letter to *The Age Good Weekend* supplement along the same lines. This letter also went unpublished. My argument was that sperm is a life-creating biological substance with significant future ramifications for the receiver's offspring and the donor alike. Donating sperm is effectively donating half the genes of one or more potential new people. Many immature young men failed to think through the consequences of their sperm donations and to appreciate that the new people created would have human rights too.

On 8 November 2014, I wrote a couple of terse letters to *The Age*. The first was in response to a further free advertisement under the guise of a topical article for sperm donation to Melbourne IVF, which bemoaned "The issue in Victoria has been the legislation, which allows identification as a right to the offspring when they turn 18." Indeed, accurate information about and maintenance of contact with one's parents are universal rights enshrined in the *UN Convention on the Rights of the Child*. It is a sad and disturbing indictment on Australian society that mainstream media has been allowed to decide that the desires of infertile prospective parents outweigh the rights of children – the most vulnerable and voiceless. The second letter was to *Good Weekend* in relation to an appalling article about a woman who, with her husband, went to California for IVF pre-implantation sex selection in order to have a baby girl. This practice is considered unethical, and is thus illegal, in Australia, except when screening for genetic disorders. Both my letters failed to make the cut. However, I was more than pleased that every one of the six letters published in the next edition of *Good Weekend* also strongly rebuked the woman who had undergone IVF pre-implantation sex selection. The *Good Weekend* letters editor noted, "Our story 'Mummy's Girl', about Jayne Cornwill's determination to have a baby daughter after giving birth to three sons, prompted a tidal wave of email."

To my great frustration throughout 2014, it also appeared that LGBTI lobbyists were using the same media tactics in Victoria as had the pro-adoption lobbyists to popularise their campaign for access to children to adopt: a flood of happy, shining stories in the mainstream media. I responded to one such article in *Sunday Life* on 25 January 2015, and my letter was published in the following edition:

Published in *Sunday Life, The Age*, Sunday, 8 February 2015

NOT ALL NURTURE

Joo-Inn Chew's engaging story about lesbian mothers ("The Other Mother", January 25) was, unfortunately, flawed by a denial of the importance of genetic ties and inheritance for children. Humans are adults for many more years than they are children and their genetic/biological links become more, rather than less, important as their lives progress. The "gay baby boom" may be revolutionising the way people think about family, but it cannot change the importance of nature as well as nurture in a person's life.

Penny Mackieson, Kew, Vic

I felt obliged to continue trying to make my point. Why was it that every adult's desires had to be upheld before the rights of children were considered? So much for children's rights being paramount in legislation. I subsequently had success with publication of another letter in the following week's edition of the *Sunday Age*:

Published in *Sunday Age*, Sunday, 15 February 2015

Kids have right to know

I endorse the government's move to uphold the rights of donor-conceived people born before 1988 – the only people in Victoria not permitted access to information about their donor fathers.

It is puzzling such access was denied in the first place, given that children's universal rights to know about and have contact with their parents were enshrined in changes to adoption legislation during the same period.

Pre-1980s adoptive parents were assured their adopted children couldn't access information about their parents due to closed adoption records. The world didn't end when adoption files were opened in 1984. The doctors who promised anonymity to sperm donors had no right to do so – their handshakes were never worth more than the rights of any future offspring or legislation.

And the donors were naïve to believe donating sperm was a simple act like donating blood, and that their offspring wouldn't want to know their fathers.

Donating sperm is effectively relinquishing a potential child – many potential children – for adoption. The children have no opportunity to provide informed consent, but must live with the consequences of their "altruistic" parents and well-meaning professionals all their lives.

Penny Mackieson, Kew

5.2 Women's magazines

The glossy feel-good articles on adoption that appear in the pages of women's magazines on a regular basis demanded that I also attempt to question their stance on adoption and reproduction. Despite their plummeting circulations in recent years, such magazines still play a role in shaping opinion on various issues. They are also key vehicles used by celebrities to win public support and gain popularity, so I knew I would have to read and respond to those publications as part of my campaign – at least occasionally.

While reading the April 2014 issue of *The Australian Women's Weekly* in a waiting room, a note on the Editor-in-Chief Helen McCabe's page caught my eye. Entitled "Adoption Update," Ms McCabe stated that her magazine was "celebrating a small but important development in our campaign to have Australia's adoption laws reformed." I knew Ms McCabe was a member of the NAAW board, so I emailed her forthrightly expressing my views about the so-called 'reform' of Australia's adoption laws under Mr Abbott. I received a brief reply from Ms McCabe two days later which indicated she had raised my concerns with the NAAW board. I wrote to Ms McCabe the same day but received no further correspondence.

An article in the July 2014 edition of *The Australian Women's Weekly* spurred me to contact the editor again. The magazine ran a long article ("The Truth behind her death") about the tragic suicide of celebrity Charlotte Dawson who had been adopted as an infant. I expressed my deep sadness and questioned the magazine's shallow unsympathetic portrayal of Ms Dawson and the antecedents of her depression. Ms Dawson would have suffered trauma as a result of being separated from her mother at birth and, consequently, she was primed to struggle with her self-esteem, identity and psychological well-being throughout her life. Compounding this, she also experienced the sudden death of her adoptive father during infancy; a poor relationship with her stepfather; sexual abuse by a neighbour; and a destructive marriage. Yet, of the seven written pages devoted to Ms Dawson's story, only two brief paragraphs referenced her difficult childhood, concluding with the breathtakingly inadequate and dismissive statement, "So her childhood was a bit of a mess." Curiously overlooked was the crucial relationship between Ms Dawson and her adoptive mother, who apparently failed to protect Ms Dawson from sexual abuse and, in its aftermath, to pursue justice and appropriate therapeutic treatment for her adopted daughter. I predicted that tragic stories like Ms Dawson's would inevitably become more frequent, given Prime Minister Tony Abbott's commitment to making intercountry adoption easier, faster and cheaper. I implored *Women's Weekly* to comprehensively explore and sensitively share with its readers relevant stories and information regarding the lifelong complexities and negatives inherent in adoption, particularly for the children.

It was not just *The Australian Women's Weekly* that received my attention. In July 2014 I also wrote to the editors of *New Idea* magazine in response to a story they ran on swimmer, Ian Thorpe, in which it was lamented that, as a gay man, he would find it difficult to adopt a child in Australia. I told *New Idea* that although I was pro-same sex marriage, I considered no adult was 'entitled' to adopt a child, irrespective of their sexual orientation, family circumstances or wealth. I made clear that Ms Furness's well-funded celebrity pro-adoption campaign prioritised the interests of prospective adoptive parents over those of vulnerable children, and that she continued to promulgate many myths. Adoption – and especially intercountry adoption – was a complex matter, and so I encouraged *New Idea* to check their facts rather than simply quote widely-held myths before next publishing an article. I received an acknowledgement email from the office manager of *New Idea* a couple of hours later, including advice that my feedback had been forwarded to the editors. No part of my letter was subsequently published by *New Idea.*

It was September when I next happened to read *New Idea* and emailed another letter:

Saturday, 6 September 2014

> It was heart-warming to read about Mary Coustas' joy on the arrival and christening of her baby daughter after a long and tragic journey to motherhood. I hope your magazine will be equally empathic in future reporting on the inevitably long and difficult journeys of children like Jamie, born via overseas donor IVF, to find their biological parent(s).

A significantly edited version of my letter was published.

Published in *New Idea*, 22 September 2014 (Issue No. 38)

> **MUM AT LAST**
>
> It was heartwarming to read about Mary Coustas' joy on the arrival and christening of her daughter after a long and tragic journey to

motherhood. I hope to read more in the future about children like Jamie, born via overseas donor IVF, and their experiences.

Penny Mackieson, Kew, Vic

I emailed *New Idea* indicating that I was highly unimpressed with the considerable liberty they had taken in editing my letter. They had distorted it to the extent that it reversed the sentiment I was seeking to express; it was a breach of my moral rights as a writer. I requested an unreserved apology and a full retraction or correction in the next edition. No apology was published in the next edition so I advised them by email that I would be seeking legal advice. That same day I received a response from the *New Idea* office manager – it was polite and included the words "we apologise." However, there was no acceptance of the validity of my concern. I sent another email telling them as much and stating that if the editors were unsure of my meaning, it would have been prudent of them to contact me for clarification before publication. Unhappy with my views having been so blatantly misrepresented, I respectfully reiterated my request for a public apology and correction in the next issue. As I received no response to that email, I felt obliged to explore how else I could pursue my grievance.

On 27 September 2014, I made an enquiry to the Australian Press Council, and was subsequently referred on to the Independent Media Council. During a follow-up phone call, it was suggested to me that I may have been too subtle in the wording of my original letter. Well, I had previously been accused of having been far too blunt with my use of language, but never too subtle! I clarified the point of my letter – that while there was an obvious positive aspect to an infertile woman eventually becoming a mother, there would be a much longer-term negative aspect for a child conceived via anonymous donor IVF treatment!

A few more phone calls later and news came that the Editor-in-Chief of *New Idea* agreed that the magazine had not done justice to honouring the intent of my letter, and was planning to print my original letter in full in the issue to be available on 20 October, with the publication date 27 October 2014. It included the following statement:

> **MUM AT LAST**
>
> *In issue 38 (NI Sept 22), we published a letter from Penny Mackieson. Penny felt this didn't represent her views exactly, so we're happy to reprint her letter here in full ...*

Though finally vindicated, I had expended considerable effort – intellectual, psychological and emotional – on holding my ground in regard to this one brief letter. Significant investment was required to resist the overwhelming practice of women's magazines to 'celebritise' and sanitise the complexities, and minimise the negatives, associated with even one story of a baby having been acquired through an ethically dubious reproductive practice. The lack of reality and honesty of women's magazines was demoralising and exhausting. Yet, this one little win also provided a glimmer of hope and I felt rewarded and energised.

The October 2014 issue of *The Australian Women's Weekly* marked the reappearance of Ms Furness. It was hard to miss as she appeared in all her celebrity make-over beauty on the glossy front cover. The article inside was written by Helen McCabe – the Editor-in-Chief, a board member of Adopt Change and personal friend of Ms Furness. Ms McCabe was blatant both in her gushing approval of Ms Furness and in her misrepresentation of the 'facts' relating to intercountry adoption. This article, rather than anything approaching news, was actually a free celebrity advertisement for Adopt Change's campaign centrepiece, National Adoption Awareness Week, coming up in November 2014. I received no response to my email questioning this sycophantic approach by a publication that is still, unfortunately, trusted by many Australian women.

Ms McCabe's article referred to Peta Credlin, the Prime

Minister's Chief of Staff, having played a key role in convincing Tony Abbott to embrace Ms Furness's pro-adoption agenda. This led me to email Peta Credlin seeking the veracity of this information. A few days later I received a forthright reply from Ms Credlin. She was greatly displeased that I had contacted her, and had copied Ms McCabe into the email she sent me. The next day I responded to Ms Credlin, without copying in Ms McCabe, providing more background and context to my concerns. In hindsight, I probably should have done that first, though I doubt it would have made any difference to the outcome. I received no further response from Ms Credlin either.

I figured my name had now been added to Ms Credlin's 'anti-adoption' list, as well as to those of *Women's Weekly* and Adopt Change. Evidently, this high-profile group of successful powerful women did not like being challenged by a lowly social worker and adoptee. The close relationships between high profile celebrities, sections of the media and the office of the most powerful person in the country, the Prime Minister, led me to reflect that what mattered most in influencing social policy under the current Coalition government was not credentials or professional expertise, but how well-connected one was. There was clearly much truth in the old adage, "it is not what you know, but who you know."

Ms Credlin had publicly described herself as "a right-wing feminist" (*The Australian Women's Weekly*, October 2014, p. 38). Until I read that, I had only ever thought about feminism as a movement grounded in socialist ideals – advocating for equality and upholding women's rights wherever they were being violated, oppressed or undermined. I had not previously thought about feminism through the broader lens of the traditional political spectrum. A feminism that advocates the rights of well-off and well-connected women to be assisted to obtain other women's children over the rights of vulnerable mostly poorer women to be supported and so able to keep their children does not seem like genuine feminism to me – incompatible in fact, more like an oxymoron.

The lead up to Adopt Change's annual National Adoption Awareness Week involved the predictably happy feel-good human interest stories about intercountry adoptive families with cute smiling children that I had come to expect in the mainstream print media, but one in particular attracted my attention. It was an article in the November 2014 issue of *The Australian Women's Weekly* about a family who had adopted three young children, twins and another child the same age, from Tanzania. The family had deliberately moved overseas for a period in order to adopt children via the expatriate Australian pathway. From my social work perspective, there were many concerns with these adoptions, including the way in which the family had 'chosen' the children themselves, rather than having undergone a matching process by accredited adoption authorities; that the children were interspersed age-wise with birth children in the family; that there were now four five-year-olds in the family; that Tanzania is not a *Hague Convention* accredited country … but worse was yet to come.

On 7 November, I read a report online in *The Sydney Morning Herald* about a morning tea for adoptive families hosted by the Prime Minister ahead of National Adoption Awareness Week. Apart from a random claim made by Mr Abbott that "adoption should take a year, rather than the current average of about five years," I was horrified to discover photos of him meeting the Tanzanian children featured in the *Women's Weekly* story. This family was being promoted by Adopt Change, and the Prime Minister, as their poster intercountry adoptive family. My fears when Mr Abbott had first announced his commitment to expanding and expediting intercountry adoption were confirmed. The proposed amendments to the *Australian Citizenship Act* in relation to intercountry adoption were yet to be passed, and the specific role of the proposed new centralised intercountry adoption service to assist Australians adopt children from overseas was yet to be clarified. However, it was increasingly apparent, despite formal lip service to the contrary, that the Australian Government was happy to laud intercountry adoption outside the framework and safeguards of the *Hague Convention* – outside the scrutiny of professional, transparent, accredited processes designed to ensure the best interests of the children – and that the mainstream media were right on board with this.

This clear example of the strong cross-promotion agendas and inter-dependencies of powerful media and politicians rankled me. Tony Abbott is dependent on the media to portray him in a favourable way to increase his popularity with the general community, and the media seeks access to such powerful people in order to increase sales of their publications or boost ratings of their broadcasts. I realised that the notion that Australian media, mainstream outlets in particular, are independent and genuinely questioning of government decisions and decision-makers is an illusion. In reality, politicians and the media are dependent on each other to such an extent they could be described as symbiotic. I was becoming convinced that my campaign would need to extend further than the media; that it would have to include politicians as well.

5.3 Politicians, policy influencers and decision makers

As well as writing emails to newspapers and magazines, I also engaged with politicians, policy influencers and decision makers. This part of my campaign primarily involved sending emails and letters but, where feasible, was supplemented with personal meetings, particularly where they intersected with my involvements with relevant organisations.

5.3.1 VANISH

The key organisation with which I have connected is VANISH, the Victorian Adoption Network for Information and Self-Help. Through my employment as a social worker, I had been aware of VANISH and its important role supporting people affected by adoption since its establishment.

VANISH is a secular community organisation funded since 1990 by the Victorian government department now known as the Department of Health and Human Services (DHHS) to provide information, search, and individual and group support services to those with an adoption experience in Victoria.[29] VANISH reaches people living in other states of Australia and overseas, and has a growing membership of more than 700 people. VANISH works with persons directly affected by local and intercountry adoption and the adoption-related community, and also with the Forgotten Australian community (former state wards and 'careleavers') and people affected by donor conception. VANISH engages with the complexity of the lived experience for members of these circles and is well informed as to the impact of trauma, persistent grief and disruptions to identity for the individuals and their families.

In early December 2013, I initiated a meeting with the Manager of VANISH, Coleen Clare, in order to formally re-connect with the VANISH community, having had no direct involvement since searching for my maternal family in 1997-1998. I volunteered my knowledge and skills from 2014 onwards when my resignation from ICAS would take effect. At the time, I had no idea how soon my offer would be called upon. In mid-January 2014, I was invited to join a working group to prepare VANISH's submission to the Commonwealth Interdepartmental Committee on Overseas Adoption established by Prime Minister Tony Abbott. I also prepared and submitted a personal ten-page response to that

29 See the VANISH website at <http://vanish.org.au/about-vanish/history-of-vanish>.

Committee. In addition, I was invited to join a VANISH delegation which met with representatives from the Department of Prime Minister and Cabinet in Canberra in February 2014 to discuss VANISH's submission. I have continued my active involvement with VANISH, including joining its Committee of Management later in 2014.

In March 2014, I attended a function held by VANISH to commemorate the first anniversary of the national bi-partisan apology to those affected by past adoption policies and practices. The anniversary was not acknowledged by the Melbourne media, despite a media release by VANISH. This confirmed to me that the significance of the National Apology for Forced Adoptions had been dumped by mainstream Australian media, and thus also from the consciousness of the broader Australian community, as a result of the diversion associated with the Prime Ministerial leadership challenge on the day of Julia Gillard's apology speech.

On 25 October, I attended a function held by VANISH to commemorate the second anniversary of the Victorian government's apology for forced adoptions and to celebrate the twenty-fifth anniversary of VANISH. Once again, despite distribution of a press release by VANISH, the event was not reported in *The Age.* One of the highlights of the event was a speech by Jenny Mikakos, then Shadow Minister for Community Services and Shadow Minister for Children in Victoria. Ms Mikakos pledged – should the Labor Party win government in the November 2014 election – to remove the unpopular contact veto and accompanying sanctions legislation for relinquishing parents which had been introduced by the Liberal-National Coalition government in its 2013 amendments to the *Adoption Act 1984.* Ms Mikakos received enthusiastic applause for her speech, which was filmed by *ABC News* – some of which, I believe, was broadcast on television later that evening.

5.3.2 World Vision

In early March 2014, I decided to approach Reverend Tim Costello, the CEO of World Vision Australia, seeking to arrange a meeting with him to discuss the issue of intercountry adoption. I raised the role of the ambassadors for World Vision, Deborra-lee Furness and her husband Hugh Jackman, in the campaign to expedite and expand intercountry adoption for Australians, and how this was at odds with the work of World Vision to support families and communities living in poverty, thus keeping families together. I received a lengthy reply in late March from World Vision's Director for Government and Mutlilaterals, which detailed the organisation's guiding principles and how these aligned with UNICEF's position. She invited me to contact World Vision's Senior Advisor on Child Protection and Trafficking in Persons, based in Sydney. I emailed the Senior Advisor, referring her to the *Report of the Interdepartmental Committee on Intercountry Adoption* (April 2014), and noting that the facts presented in the Report debunked the negative myths Ms Furness had long promulgated about the way in which Australia's intercountry adoption program operated. I also requested a meeting, which the Senior Advisor referred to her Melbourne-based colleague who managed World Vision's relationship with Ms Furness.

On 22 May 2014, I had a long telephone conversation with World Vision's Ambassador Program Manager. He explained that World Vision has 14 ambassadors, including Ms Furness and Mr Jackman; that they are 'voluntary ambassadors'; that World Vision has had a long-term ongoing relationship with them; and that World Vision is the beneficiary of one of Ms Furness's charities. He further explained that World Vision does not try to be exclusive but to partner with different people, and accepts that its ambassadors will work with other charities. In his answers to my pointed questions, he articulated that he did not see any conflict of interest between Ms Furness and Mr Jackman's work with World Vision and the federal government's embrace of Ms Furness's pro-adoption agenda in relation to its 'reform' of intercountry adoption.

I followed up by sending the Ambassador Program Manager an article written by Ms Furness[30] in which she suggested re-routing money allocated for foreign aid to supporting parents who adopt children from overseas, and subsidising agencies in the private sector in order to expedite intercountry adoptions. I reiterated my concern about Ms Furness's pro-adoption agenda in relation to vulnerable children, both overseas and in Australia. The Ambassador Program Manager replied promptly, asserting that there are different views within Australia around adoption reform; respecting my right to my view based on my experience and work history; and respecting the right of Ms Furness and Mr Jackman to have their view as well. He stated that overseas adoption is not an advocacy priority for World Vision at this time.

What did I make of all that? Well, I considered World Vision Australia's brush-off to be one of the nicest I had ever received from a big bureaucracy. However, I was far from satisfied with their response to my concerns, particularly in relation to the enmeshment of the 'voluntary' ambassadorial relationship Ms Furness and Mr Jackman enjoyed with World Vision. It was very clear that World Vision was happy to benefit financially from one of Ms Furness's charities and from the media promotion inherent in its association with Ms Furness and Mr Jackman in exchange for the philanthropic kudos for the ambassadors through their involvement with that international aid agency. Another old adage came to mind: "I'll scratch your back if you scratch mine." I was bemused that World Vision could be so publicly concerned about the exploitation of vulnerable children for the purposes of labour or sex, yet apparently unconcerned about the exploitation of the same vulnerable children for the purposes of intercountry adoption. It seemed akin to the apparent hypocrisy of the

30 See Jackman (2011).

Abbott government in relation to adoption. What was it about adoption that made otherwise intelligent people blind to the inherent opportunities for exploitation?

In July 2014, I wrote again to World Vision Australia's CEO. I recapped my concerns and also indicated my disappointment that his organisation did not include trafficking of children for the purposes of intercountry adoption as a social justice issue, alongside trafficking for the purposes of labour or sexual exploitation, particularly given that the former also exploited young women and children living in poverty. I received no reply to my letter.

In September 2014, I sent another letter to World Vision Australia – this time an even more uncomfortable one – terminating the sponsorships for two children which my husband and I had maintained for more than 20 years. I advised that our decision was based on my deep concerns regarding the ongoing ambassadorships of Ms Furness and her husband with World Vision; and that I was very uncomfortable with the conflict of interest inherent in supporting the work of an organisation that has ambassadors with a misguided agenda that runs counter to the best interests of the very children in overseas countries that the organisation seeks to support. On noticing a few weeks later that a further monthly sponsorship payment had been withdrawn from our credit card account, I phoned World Vision in October. I learned that although World Vision had received my letter, they had not acted on it. They cited significant backlogs as the reason for this.

5.3.3 Politicians

I also felt it was important to convey my concerns regarding the Australian government's intercountry adoption policy to my local representative in federal Parliament. So, in early March 2014 I initiated contact with Josh Frydenberg, my local Federal Member and Parliamentary Secretary to the Prime Minister with responsibility for the government's deregulation agenda. Our subsequent half-hour meeting on 9 May was cut short due to Mr Frydenberg's late arrival, so I felt obliged to launch into outlining my issues more directly than I had planned. Mr Frydenberg admitted this was not the first time someone from his electorate had raised with him concerns about Mr Abbott's endeavours in relation to intercountry adoption. In the subsequent days, I sent Mr Frydenberg two lengthy letters, thanking him for hearing my concerns; recapping and clarifying the points we had discussed; and requesting that he convey those concerns to his colleagues.

I received a very polite letter back from him in early June 2014 containing information from various government websites and from the *Report of the Interdepartmental Committee on Overseas Adoption* (April 2014), of which I was already well aware. Mr Frydenberg thanked me for meeting with him and for my subsequent correspondence. He indicated that he would bring my "latest correspondence to the Prime Minister's attention." Reading between the lines of bureaucratic politeness, I felt sure Mr Frydenberg and his government could not have cared less about my views on intercountry adoption.

The only piece of new information provided by Mr Frydenberg was that "on 2 January 2014 the Prime Minister wrote to around 20 major stakeholders that represented a range of views." This small number surprised me, as I could list about 20 major stakeholders in the adoption field in Victoria alone and I knew that VANISH was not among those the Prime Minister had approached. I wrote back to Mr Frydenberg asking for the list of selected organisations but did not receive a reply – well, not for several months, anyway. The 'range of views' was evidently highly selective and only represented the pro-adoption perspective.

In May, I sent a six-and-a-half-page letter outlining the concerns I had raised with Mr Frydenberg to 20 other people – state and federal members of parliament, senators, and two key Victorian out-of-home care providers. I received responses from ten of them, the last on 6 August 2014.[31]

The first response I received was from Colleen Hartland, Greens Member of State Parliament for the Western Suburbs and Victorian Greens Spokesperson for Community Services. Her brief letter noted that intercountry adoption was a federal issue and that I had also sent my letter to the Greens spokesperson, Senator Sarah Hanson-Young. In Australian football parlance, this represented a handpass.

The second reply was from the Assistant Director of the Victorian Department of Premier and Cabinet, presumably on behalf of the Premier, Dr Denis Napthine, though it did not specifically say so. This letter was also very brief, stating that the matter was a federal one and advising that my letter had been forwarded to the Department of Prime Minister and Cabinet for a response. Another handpass.

The third reply was from Megan Mitchell, the National Children's Commissioner, Australian Human Rights Commission. Ms Mitchell acknowledged that I had raised "a range of very important concerns and issues regarding current intercountry adoption program developments" and advised that she would "raise the concerns ... with [her] colleagues in the Australian Children's Commissioners and Guardians group" and in her regular meetings with Members of Parliament and government officials. At last, the sort of response I had been seeking! A commitment to speaking to others. In Australian football terms, this was equivalent to a mark inside the forward 50-metre zone.

31 Those from whom I did not receive a response included: Daniel Andrews (Victorian Leader of the Opposition); Geoff Shaw (Victorian Member for Frankston); Kevin Andrews (Federal Minister for Social Services); Doug Cameron (Federal Shadow Minister for Human Services, Senate); Jenny Macklin (Federal Shadow Minister for Families and Payments); Cathy McGowan (Federal Member for Indi); Andrew Wilkie (Federal member for Denison); Sarah Hanson-Young (Federal Senator, Greens); the Principal Commissioner for Children and Young People, Victoria; and the CEO of Anglicare.

The fourth reply was a one-page letter signed by the Victorian Parliamentary Secretary for Families and Community Services on behalf of the Minister for Community Services, Mary Wooldridge. It outlined "the Commonwealth's significant role in intercountry adoption and their Attorney-General's role in leading the negotiation of Australia's relationship with partner countries since 2008." There was no new information: "At this stage no decision about the model or agencies to be involved have been made." There was nothing to indicate that the Napthine government cared whether, how or by whom the intercountry adoption program would be delivered in Victoria in the future. In footy speak, this was a ball-up scenario.

I received the fifth and sixth replies the same day. One was from the office of Christine Milne, Senator for Tasmania and Leader of the Australian Greens. This letter thanked me for my "input on this complex issue" and stated that "The Australian Greens remain wary about any change to adoption policies and urge the utmost caution" and that "it is critical that any legislation to make adoptions easier must have adequate safeguards to ensure that we do not repeat the mistakes of the past." The other reply was from the CEO of Berry Street, stating that their organisation shared similar concerns to mine regarding the proposed changes to intercountry adoption. From a footy perspective, these two could be considered fellow club members.

The seventh reply was a brief letter from the Family Policy Section, Department of Immigration and Border Protection, presumably on behalf of Scott Morrison who was then the Minister for Immigration and Border Protection, though it did not specifically state this. A curious three-word slogan at the bottom of the letter caught my eye – it read, "**people** our business". Ironically, it seemed like proof of the commodification of vulnerable children and people from overseas by the Australian Government. The letter noted that I had met with "the Department of the Prime Minister and

Cabinet and the Prime Minister's Parliamentary Secretary, the Hon Josh Frydenberg MP, to discuss [my] concerns and that [I] have also written to and received a reply from Mr Frydenberg." I felt like the umpire was determined to impress on me that he was in charge of this game and that, even though he could hear my barracking from the outer, nothing I said would make any difference to when, or for what, he would blow his whistle. I was increasingly convinced that the Australian Government would be happy if it never heard from me again on the subject of intercountry adoption. Jolly bad luck for them!

The eighth reply was perhaps the most disappointing, as I had expected a great deal more. This letter was from the Office of the Leader of the Opposition, Bill Shorten, but was neither named nor signed by anyone. Notwithstanding, the letter stated "between now and the next election in 2016, Labor will consider opinions such as yours carefully in developing a range of policies and plans for Australia." But my heart sank when I read "inter-country adoption can be a long, time consuming and difficult process, and the Prime Minister's changes may streamline this process." Continuing the football analogy, it appeared that the Office of the Leader of the Opposition was hedging its bets regarding which team it would barrack for in this particular game. However, it was also clear that the Office of the Leader of the Opposition was unconcerned about the commitments made in Labor Prime Minister Julia Gillard's national apology in March 2013 to the thousands of Australians adversely affected by past unethical adoption practices.

The ninth reply was from Jenny Mikakos, Shadow Minister for Children and Shadow Minister for Community Services in Victoria. Ms Mikakos affirmed "it is vital that Australia's inter-country adoption program is regulated to make sure that any adoption is in the best interests of the children affected," and stated she "will give consideration to the need for a review of the Victorian Adoption Act and to the matters [I] raised in

[my] letter." This response was clear, positive and, in AFL[32] lingo, made me feel like the Laws of the Game Committee had registered the problem; acknowledged the need to comprehensively review it; and would take corrective action at the earliest opportunity.

Finally, I received a reply from Richard Marles, Shadow Immigration and Border Protection Minister. Mr Marles stated that

> Labor supports the amendments and the general objectives of the Bill,[33] however, we understand that it is critical to ensure that, despite the best intentions of the bill, there are not unintended consequences, namely the risk that any change to the current framework may put children at risk of being trafficked ... It must be ensured that stringent safeguards are put in place to prevent this from happening ... Intercountry adoption should be about finding families for children, not children for families.

I felt Mr Marles definitely understood my concerns. That is, right up until I read: "be assured that Labor will keep the government to account in regards to this program." That was the very point! I did not feel assured, particularly given the response I had received earlier from the Office of the Leader of the Opposition. In football terms, this felt about as reassuring as if an umpire who had not bothered to put on his spectacles said, "Trust me: I'm an umpire."

In the midst of receiving responses from my May 2014 twenty-letter campaign, I learned that the Abbott government had introduced to parliament the *Australian Citizenship Amendment (Intercountry Adoption) Bill 2014*. The Bill was purportedly to allow immediate granting of Australian citizenship to children adopted in South Korea and Taiwan,

32 Australian Football League: the most popular code of elite football in Australia.

33 Presumably this was in reference to the proposed *Australian Citizenship Amendment (Intercountry Adoption) Bill 2014*.

countries with which Australia had bilateral arrangements rather than *Hague Convention*-to-*Hague Convention* intercountry adoption programs. However, there was potential for this amendment to make it much easier for expatriate Australians to adopt children in other countries not party to the *Hague Convention* – whether those countries were unable or unwilling to ratify it – should the Australian Government develop further bilateral agreements. Thus, on 2 June 2014, I sent a terse email to the Prime Minister expressing my concerns. I received a letter back the next day from the Ministerial and Parliamentary Support Branch advising that the Prime Minister had referred my correspondence to the Attorney-General for a response.

I subsequently received a response, dated 7 July 2014, from the Assistant Secretary, Marriage and Intercountry Adoption, Attorney-General's Department, which referred to my email of 2 June to the Prime Minister; my letter of 19 May to the Minister for Social Services, Kevin Andrews; and my meeting in May with Josh Frydenberg, and subsequent exchange of correspondence with him. The letter stated that

> ... as a signatory to the Hague Convention, the Australian Government is committed to ensuring that any reform is consistent with the core principles of the Hague Convention that intercountry adoptions are arranged in the best interest of the child with respect to his or her fundamental rights.

Reading between the polite weasel words, the letter from the Attorney-General's Department confirmed that asserting a commitment to "the core principles of the Hague Convention that intercountry adoptions are arranged in the best interest of the child" was not the same as being fully committed to all the ethical and legal requirements of the *Hague Convention*, nor to a child-focussed interpretation of "best interest of the child." After all, Deborra-lee Furness called herself a 'child advocate', yet she was tunnel-visioned in her view that adoption was in the best interests of a child, contrary to decades of extensive research findings which indicate that separation of a child from his or her family of origin will have lifelong negative impacts.

In early December 2014, I received another letter from Josh Frydenberg, which advised that he "was recently provided with a copy of a letter to [me] from [the] Assistant Secretary for Marriage and Intercountry Adoption in the Attorney-General's Department responding to [my] earlier correspondence to the Prime Minister, the Hon Tony Abbott and the Minister for Social Services, the Hon Kevin Andrews MP." Evidently, the Commonwealth ministerial correspondence management system was working well. Mr Frydenberg described the letter from the Attorney-General's Department as a

> comprehensive response [addressing] the proposed changes to intercountry adoption reform, emphasising compliance with international obligations through bilateral agreements. The Australian Government is committed to ensuring that any reform in this area is consistent with the core Australia's international legal obligations under the Hague Convention.

Aside from some poor wording suggestive of hasty composition, I was intrigued at having been sent another letter from Mr Frydenberg some five months since my last correspondence to him. There was nothing new in his response and it did not address my request to be provided with the list of 20 'major stakeholders' invited by the Prime Minister in January 2014 to make submissions in regard to his proposed reforms to intercountry adoption. If anything, this letter served to heighten my concerns that the government was more focussed on compliance with bilateral agreements than compliance with the *Hague Convention.* I considered that a copy of this letter would make a neat addition to the ASIO file which I fondly imagined was being maintained about me.

On Monday 9 February 2015 – late in the evening of the first day of sitting in the New Year – the Senate passed the Abbott government's proposed *Australian Citizenship Amendment (Intercountry Adoption) Bill.* Yet, this news was not announced in *The Age*, nor in any of the other mainstream Australian newspapers. I was unsuccessful in getting any of my indignant letters on the subject published in *The Age* midweek – I imagined that, perhaps, the letters editor had finally banned me altogether.

5.4 Other media

During the course of my campaign, my networks in the adoption/donor conception/surrogacy space invariably also expanded, and opportunities to present my perspective and positions in media other than print arose. For example, I was interviewed in late 2014 and again in early 2015 for a documentary on adoption in Australia, 'As If Born To', being made by Pascal Huynh, a young Canadian filmmaker. Subsequent to this, I participated in a number of online panel discussions hosted by Pascal which explored the sustainability of adoption in Australia.[34] In April 2015 I was interviewed by ABC-TV reporter, Louise Milligan, for a story highlighting the complexities and negative aspects of adoption which was subsequently broadcast on the *7.30* program on 4 June 2015.[35]

Conclusion

I admit that sometimes it has felt like all I have done since resigning from ICAS at the end of 2013 is read *The Age* from cover-to-cover each morning, then copy-and-paste terse letters and articles and email them to the editors in response to adoption, donor conception and/or surrogacy issues that have disturbed me. Indeed, an awful lot has disturbed and aggrieved me, to the extent that my husband has expressed concern that I

34 See Huynh for full references to the online panel discussions. The documentary is due for completion in November 2015, when it is to be submitted to human rights film festivals, including here in Australia.

35 See Milligan (2015).

have changed – that I have become 'an angry person'. I do not like this new persona very much, but I am not ready to divest myself of my passion either, for it is a precious fuel not to be wasted. In my own defence, I believe I would have already imploded as a result of the social injustices I perceived if I were not channelling my anger and commitment into relevant, and hopefully also constructive, counter activities.

CHAPTER 6

Where to from here for adoption in Australia?

In Australia it is evident that the struggle for recognising and upholding the rights of vulnerable children and their mothers and families has been going on for a long time. This has been proven time and again, even when generations of such children become adults. As Professor Shurlee Swain (2012, p. 1) has noted:

> Adoption has a long history in Australia, in which the 'boom' years of 1940-1975 constitute a minor portion. As a social practice, it has been driven by several forces, sometimes competing, sometimes complementary: the problem of the unsupported child, the moral disgrace associated with pregnancy outside marriage, the desire for a child and the pressure on professionals to satisfy that desire, all functioning to introduce elements of the market into a field that masqueraded as benevolent. Each reform was constituted as a dramatic break with an evil past which needed to be set aside.

There has long been a preference by government decision-makers to separate children from their families when children's needs are not being, or *may* not be, adequately met. Too hastily they are placed in alternative care arrangements, before investigating and investing in different ways to provide additional or more effective ongoing support to the families. Unfortunately for the children, it is far easier to remove them from sub-optimal situations than change their parents' situations, despite the knowledge that this practice inflicts trauma on the children for their parents' perceived failings, as well as on the parents themselves. It will be interesting to see whether this approach changes with the growing commitment in Australia to better address domestic violence – which constitutes a significant social problem; a major cause of injuries, health impacts and deaths, especially women's; and a major factor contributing to the removal of children by child protection programs.[36] Hopefully, the awarding of the 2015 Australian of the Year to Rosie Batty has marked the beginning of a genuine and broad-based approach to improving measures to prevent family breakdowns, rather than third party exploitation of such circumstances.

In Australia it is also evident that adult adoptees are often treated as if we were still children – as if "frozen in time," as so aptly described by Thomas Graham, the founder and editor of the Australian Journal of Adoption[37] (2014, p. 22) – and thus as if we do not have voices of our own. If people concede that we progress beyond childhood, they often discount our adult voices – as if our perspective is somehow invalid; as if we should forever feel lucky and be grateful for having been adopted; as if we have no right to question the decisions that were made regarding who should raise us. It is far too easily forgotten that *adoption is always forced on the children, but the consequences impact the adults that the children become for the entirety of our lives.*

There is ongoing strong demand by prospective parents for a supply of healthy infants to form or complete their families. And so the lopsided conflict of interest between the rights

36 See Department of Reproductive Health and Research, World Health Organization (2013); and Phillips and Vandenbroek (2014).

37 The *Australian Journal of Adoption* is an independent, free, online community resource for people affected by, or involved, in adoption in Australia and New Zealand <http://www.nla.gov.au/openpublish/index.php/aja/index>.

of vulnerable children and the perceived rights of intending parents is constantly manipulated, distorted and undermined by the latter, inherently more powerful, group. Social workers have all too frequently found themselves caught up in these tensions – like an earlier version of myself, taking a pragmatic stance. As Dr Patricia Fronek and Professor Denise Cuthbert (2013, pp. 408–409) have observed:

> The important question to be debated is how social workers can be supported to move past purely pragmatic positions to influence policy and practice at structural levels where families are disadvantaged, and communities depleted of their children because lesser standards are accepted for people elsewhere to meet the interests of lobbyists and claim-makers in Australia …

Still, I am alarmed at the breathtaking speed and ease with which both domestic and intercountry adoption have been sugar-coated and re-popularised since the bi-partisan national apology of March 2013. Rescuing children who are 'languishing' in 'orphanages' and foster care placements is pushed emotively and relentlessly by powerful lobbyists, right-wing think-tanks and mainstream media alike on a gullible and uninformed public. It is presented as the best and most altruistic solution to meeting the needs of vulnerable children living in poverty in Third World countries, or in overburdened domestic child protection systems. 'Love' is shallowly touted as a sufficient prerequisite to parent such children and as sufficient reason to justify permanently separating them from their families and communities of origin. And this happens despite the fact that the majority of people who express interest in adopting a child are, in fact, not suitable to take on this complex lifelong commitment. Indeed, if love were all that was required to parent a child well, it would be an extremely rare occurrence for a child to be removed from their family for reasons of child protection. I know from my professional employment with Victoria's community services programs that the vast majority of parents deeply love their children, even when found to have been neglectful or abusive towards them.

Similarly, I am alarmed at the way in which overseas anonymous donor IVF and commercial surrogacy have been popularised. These practices are promoted as bringing invaluable joy to people desperate to form their own families and otherwise unable to do so, despite the fact that they are currently banned for ethical reasons in all states and territories of Australia bar the Northern Territory, which has no relevant laws. More importantly, there is simply no right to a child – especially not when the act of procuring that child is based on the exploitation of a destitute or disadvantaged woman or family. It is not rocket science to grasp that, while it is every child's right to be adequately parented, parenthood is not the right of every adult – and definitely not parenthood by whatever means it takes.

The rights of the most vulnerable people are being overridden and their circumstances exploited. Expert credibility is being wilfully ignored by government decision-makers, replaced with economically-driven think-tanks and well-connected lobbyists. As prospective adopters have become more desperate and adoption policy more political, social workers – the key professionals in child and family welfare – are being sidelined from the complex processes that determine whether and when a child should be removed from their mother/parents and with which alternative parents the child should be raised. And all of this is happening even before the dust has settled on the damage done to previous generations adversely affected by mass family separation practices. It is as if there is a collective and wilful amnesia in regard to the lessons from the recent apologies for the poor child welfare policies and practices of Australia's past. As Swain has concluded (2012, p. 11):

> Politicians and media commentators are apt to talk about learning from history. As a historian I would caution that the only lesson from history is that at any point in time there are multiple possible

> ways to proceed. The 'problems' that adoption was designed to solve, particularly the need to provide economically for children, and the pain of infertility, are still with us today and 'best interests' remains, ostensibly, the primary principle in the development of solutions. However … 'best interests' are not as obvious or transparent as those who argue for any single solution at any point in time might suppose, and … the decisions we make will have consequences that we cannot foresee.

I cannot help but empathise with intercountry adoptees – they must deal with losing their country, culture and language in addition to their name, identity and family of origin. Similarly, I cannot help but empathise with anonymous donor conceived people, and people born overseas via commercial surrogacy. Many of them may never be able to discover their full biological origins or have the opportunity to know their genetic and/or birth parents. This situation will only be exacerbated as a result of the passing in February 2015 of the Abbott government's *Australian Citizenship Amendment (Intercountry Adoption) Bill*, which will facilitate unregulated expatriate adoptions of children overseas.

Many Australians adopted from overseas who are now adults feel constrained by expectations, overt or perceived, from their adoptive families to express gratitude or, at least, to not express anything that could be interpreted as ingratitude or disloyalty. Few such people dare risk their relationships with their adoptive families by speaking publicly or freely about adoption in anything other than glowing, or at worst neutral, terms. Even fewer dare to discuss the complexities of their identities and family relationships; the racism they invariably experienced while growing up in Australia with white parents; or the anecdotally high rates of suicide in their intercountry adoptee networks.[38] Thomas Graham found that, while

38 For example, Sophie English and Le My Huong, intercountry adoptees from Vietnam, told their stories on the *ABC's Foreign Correspondent* program on 21 April 2015 <http://www.abc.net.au/foreign/content/2015/s4220901.htm>.

there are no large-scale or longitudinal research projects on suicide in Australia involving adopted people, "international research has shown that adopted people are statistically more likely to engage in suicide behaviour than their non-adopted counterparts" (Graham, 2014, p. 19). There is every reason to believe that the findings from the international studies to which Graham refers are applicable to the Australian context: for example, a Swedish study found that intercountry adoptees were 4.5 times more likely to attempt suicide than the general population, and 3.6 times more likely to die from suicide (in Graham, 2014, p. 5).

I no longer risk upsetting or offending my adoptive parents as they are both deceased. I am thus well positioned to speak publicly about the complexities of adoption – the complexities that the mainstream media are reticent to highlight, enamoured as they are with the positive human interest stories associated with fulfillment of prospective parents' long and difficult journeys to parenthood.

It amazes me that mainstream media in this country can vehemently object to the inhumanity and cruelty of the Australian government's asylum seeker policies, particularly for children, yet not comprehend that the recent developments in adoption policy and the reproductive technology industry – developments which it apparently supports – also violate the universal human rights of the world's most vulnerable people. *Children are not merely entitled to be raised by a mother and a father. Children are entitled to be raised by, or at least to have ongoing relationships with or know about, their own mother and their own father* – the mother from whose body and womb they were born, and the mother and father from whose gametes they were created.

I cannot in good conscience sit idly by while the retrograde neo-liberal ruling class engineers a renaissance of the destructive age of unethical adoption in Australia, and turns a blind eye to the new age of unethical third party reproduction in the global commercialised baby market. I cannot abide the systematic creation of yet more traumatised generations of Australians deliberately deprived of their true identities and relationships with their families of origin for the selfish purposes of the infertile bourgeoisie who consider having children their 'entitlement'.

On 12 November 2014, I attended a presentation, 'Forced adoption: Righting wrongs of a dark past', held by the Australian Institute of Family Studies (the Australian Government's key research body in the area of family well-being). The guest speaker was Professor The Honourable Nahum Mushin – the former Chair of the Australian Government's Forced Adoption Apology Reference Group and, following that, the Chair of the Australian Government's Forced Adoption Implementation Working Group. Professor Mushin openly stated his opinion that a national apology was overdue for people from overseas affected by unethical practices associated with past intercountry adoptions by Australian citizens. I fervently hope to witness that apology in the not too distant future, in anticipation that it will also include people affected by the Australian government's current misguided endeavours to expedite and expand the number of intercountry adoptions.

Professor Mushin also indicated his concern that *integrated birth certificates* may be the one and only recommendation of the 20 recommendations made by the Forced Adoption Apology Reference Group that would *not* have been implemented, or at least be in progress, by the time the Forced Adoption Implementation Working Group wound up at the end of December 2014. It is no exaggeration to state that a key part of my identity and ongoing psychological well-being is invested in the realisation of that particular recommendation.

An *integrated birth certificate* is a birth certificate that would include accurate information about a person's birth, as registered usually by the mother soon after her child's birth, as well as about the child's changed legal status and identity upon adoption. In other words, an integrated birth certificate would link the child's original – or true – identity with their adoptive identity and include identifying details for both sets of parents, birth and adoptive, in one and the same legal document.

I am aware that not all adopted people would want such a document if it were available to them, but I am one of the many who do. I question the point of having an identity document that does not accurately reflect one's identity. I feel no shame for having been adopted, so why should I have to continue the charade of invisibility regarding my family origins? If adoption practices are truly open now, why should my primary identity document continue to mask the facts of my parentage? Why should the general community not be reminded of one of the key injustices of adoption every time I am required to provide my birth certificate as proof of my identity?

On 25 August 2014, I posted a Freedom of Information (FOI) application to Monash Health in order to seek, once and for all, any medical records relating to my birth and subsequent hospitalisation. I first enquired back in 1990, after I had successfully applied for, and received, my adoption records. At that time, the Queen Victoria Hospital (QVH) had already merged with the Monash Hospital, but I was unsuccessful in my attempt to engage with anyone able – or, perhaps, willing? – to guide me through the process of applying for my QVH records. In hindsight, I believe I was given the brush off. In any event, I received a letter dated 26 August 2014 confirming receipt of my application. I received a subsequent letter dated 22 September indicating the mixed outcome of my request:

> It was my intention to grant your request in full however after an extensive search of our patient information databases I have been unable to locate a medical record belonging to either you or your mother. Public Record Office guidelines at the time would have allowed for destruction of the medical record. Birth registers must

> be kept permanently and I am able to give you a copy of the line in the birth register that refers to the birth episode.

In response, I then wrote to the Freedom of Information Commissioner to complain, under Section 61A(I) of the FOI Act, that I had been unable to access records relating to my birth at QVH in Melbourne due to the apparent destruction of my medical records by that hospital. I expressed my extreme disappointment with the lack of available information regarding my birth at QVH – *medical records from the first 3 weeks of my life as a hospital in-patient reduced to a one-line "birth episode"!* I noted it was bad enough that policy makers at the time considered it not only acceptable, but desirable, to force the adoption of babies like me born to young mothers out of wedlock. But now I had discovered that administrators at the time considered it acceptable, and probably also desirable, to destroy relevant records pertaining to their ethically dubious practices! I stated that it had been almost two years since the Victorian government formally apologised to those affected by the forced adoption practices in this state between the 1950s and 1970s. Yet when, if ever, could I expect to achieve a sense of healing from the injustice and cruelty of those practices given the thoughtlessness and insensitivity associated with the destruction of my precious medical records?

I subsequently received a number of phone calls from the FOI Commission officer assigned to deal with my complaint, and also had a phone conversation with a senior staff member of the Southern Health (now Monash Health) FOI Unit in which she explained the comprehensive process her staff had employed in searching for my QVH records. I followed up with an email to the FOI Commission officer confirming the content of my phone conversation with the Southern Health FOI representative. I also expressed that, while I accepted there was nothing further anyone could do to resurrect my records, I was deeply hurt and unhappy with the situation.

Further, I outlined my grave concerns in relation to the possibility of the reintroduction of practices that would allow destruction of hospital records in cases similar to mine in the future, given recent policy and legislative developments in adoption at both the state and federal levels.

Meanwhile on 15 September 2014, I attended the Births Deaths and Marriages (BDM) office in Collins Street, Melbourne, where I was required to hand in my 'Sixth Schedule' (the special birth certificate issued for adoptees like me, which I had possessed since my teenage years) when I applied for my legal birth certificate. At the same time, I also applied for a new copy of my original birth certificate. Two days later I received via post my two new birth certificates. The information included on them was, of course, exactly as I had expected. On my original certificate, Carol was recorded as my mother; there was no entry in the section for my father; and my identifying details included the names Carol gave me upon my birth. On my legal birth certificate, my adoptive parents were recorded as my mother and father; I was identified by the names my adoptive parents gave me; and there was nothing to link the identity of 'Lisa Jane Smith' with 'Penelope Kathleen Mackieson', apart from 'Sex: Female, 'Date of Birth: 10 March 1963' and two big red 'CANCELLED' stamps.

On 18 September 2014, I wrote to the Director and Registrar of BDM to request that a new, more accurate and *integrated*, birth certificate be issued for me. In my letter I explained that Carol was, and would always be, my biological and genetic mother; that her name and details appeared correctly on my original birth certificate; and that administrative 'cancellation' of my birth registration upon my adoption did not and could never change the accuracy of this fact. I further explained that the names and details of my adoptive parents appear on my legal birth certificate as my 'Mother' and 'Father', as if they were my birth/biological/genetic parents. However, this is obviously incorrect as I have only one birth/biological/genetic mother, despite registration of her details being cancelled by BDM and that the details of my biological/genetic father were not registered at the time of my birth. I reiterated that Mum and Dad are my adoptive/social/legal parents, and that they would continue to be so, despite the fact that they are now both deceased.

I further explained that, from my perspective as an adopted person directly affected by the pre-1980s policies and practices of forced and closed adoption in Victoria, my birth history comprises a significant part of my identity. And from my perspective as a social worker of 30 years' experience in children and family services – including almost 12 years with DHS's intercountry adoption program – it is vital from social, biological/genetic and legal perspectives that a person's birth certificate be accurate. As my legal birth certificate is clearly not accurate, it represents an ongoing dissonance in my adoption journey, which I am very keen to heal. I thus outlined my request for reissue of my legal birth certificate in a format that includes all the relevant registered information. While I noted that I am not seeking to also have my biological father's name and details included on my birth certificate at this time, I clarified that this does not mean I do not consider it appropriate. After all, the facts of my birth are the facts of my birth: Carol has verified the identity of my father and he did not deny my paternity when he discovered my existence or, later, when we had our one and only conversation via phone. However, I have continued to feel torn about adding my father's details to my birth certificate – even if it were possible – without him being able to provide his specific consent for this. I acknowledge that I may well feel differently if my paternal aunt were to acknowledge me.

I advised that I had given this matter much consideration over many years. Also, that I knew amendments had been made in 2013 to the *Adoption Act 1984* which allowed BDM "to enable a birth certificate to be issued for a child adopted in a [Hague] Convention country, whose adoption is recognised under section 69D of the [Adoption] Act" (*Adoption Amendment Act 2013*, p. i), and that considerable work had been undertaken to ensure the details included on such new birth certificates were as accurate as possible. I stated it was not my fault I was adopted, and nor my choice for a vital part of my identity to be wiped away with a red 'CANCELLED' stamp. I thus sought the Registrar's support and assistance in having my legal birth certificate updated and integrated to accurately reflect the records pertaining to my birth, and thus to reflect my true family history and identity.

On 13 October 2014, I received a reply from BDM regarding my request for an integrated birth certificate.

> The Registrar regrets that the issuance of an integrated birth certificate is currently not possible [because] in February 2012, the Senate Community Affairs References Committee into former forced adoption policies and practices submitted a report that recommended harmonisation of records relating to forced adoption. Implementation of the recommendation is currently not possible in Victoria without legislative amendment. The Registrar will raise this matter with the Attorney General as part of a proposal to amend the *Births Deaths and Marriages Registration Act 1996.*

On 23 October, I sent an email to the then Attorney-General of Victoria, Robert Clark.[39] I sought advice regarding the details and timeframe of an amendment to the *Births Deaths and Marriages Registration Act 2006*, as referred to in the letter from BDM and as per Recommendation 13 of the Commonwealth

39 I copied the email to Martin Pakula (then Shadow Attorney-General for Victoria), Jenny Mikakos (then Shadow Minister for Community Services), George Brandis (the Commonwealth Attorney-General), Mark Dreyfus (the Commonwealth Shadow Attorney-General), Claire Moore (Labor Senator for Queensland), Rachel Siewert (Greens Senator for Western Australia) and Nahum Mushin (Adjunct Professor of Law at Monash University).

Senate Community Affairs References Committee Inquiry into Former Forced Adoption Policies and Practices:

> That all jurisdictions adopt integrated birth certificates, that these be issued to eligible people upon request, and that they be legal proof of identity of equal status to other birth certificates.

I did not receive a reply to that letter, and nor did I expect to do so after the State elections of 29 November 2014 when Mr Clark's party failed to win re-election to government.

However, on 2 February 2015, I received a promising letter from Martin Pakula, the new Andrews Labor government's Attorney-General:

> I have ... asked my Department to work through the policy and operational matters regarding the future production of an integrated certificate as a proof of identity document. These include issues arising from the recording of two identities on a birth certificate, potential confusion about the adoptee's 'legal identity' and the current ability of the Document Verification Service to verify an adoptee's post-adoption birth certificate only.
>
> The production and use of an integrated birth certificate are matters under consideration for legislative reform, amongst other, civil registration issues.
>
> Thank you for drawing this important matter to the Attorney-General's attention.

In conclusion, I believe it is delusional in this day and age – particularly in this state – for any mature, intelligent and informed adult to hold that adoption is in a child's best interests. Adoption is a broken and obsolete concept. Government decision-makers knew this to be the case when the current *Adoption Act* was introduced in Victoria in 1984. And when *Permanent Care Orders* were introduced in 1992, adoption should have been done away with altogether. That adoption has continued to be considered by some to hold an important place in child welfare policy in Victoria reflects the continuing existence of a pro-adoption culture among a small group of social workers and community services agencies historically influential in regard to child protection and out-of-home care policies in this state.

The current crop of celebrity do-gooders may be able to convince both themselves and the general community that promoting adoption is the height of humanitarianism and altruism in regard to children, but I am not so gullible. I know firsthand that love is mandatory but not sufficient for effective care and parenting of an adopted child – whether born locally or overseas. As a social worker with ICAS it was a pleasure to work with families who 'got' that adoptive parenting requires sound motivations and realistic and flexible expectations, rather than idealistic dreams. It also requires a genuine, rather than selectively, non-racist and non-judgmental attitude. Applicants who understood and accepted all of this also appreciated that adoption is a lifelong journey for all parties involved, which is not 'finalised' with the signing of the legal adoption paperwork.

From my perspective, genuine child advocates would never advocate for adoption. They would appreciate that *being forcibly separated from one's family of origin is a violation of a child's rights of such magnitude that it should never be compounded by additionally violating the child's rights to their identity and ongoing legal connections with their parents and extended family.* They would acknowledge that adoption orders will always favour the interests of the adoptive parents at the expense of the children and their families of origin, and would work towards adoption being a thing of the past. In Victoria, genuine child advocates would focus on overcoming the systemic difficulties in the out-of-home care system and the resourcing deficits which have hampered best practice implementation of Permanent Care Orders.[40]

My perspective on adoption and other third party

40 In August 2015, I commenced PhD studies with the School of Social Work at the University of Melbourne with a focus on the history, purpose and outcomes of Permanent Care Orders in Victoria.

reproduction is a logical extension of my own lived experience, together with testimonies and research findings from thousands of people who were adopted or born of donor conception during the last half century. I have already been an adult for much longer than I was a child in the direct care of my adoptive parents, and the complexities of my adoption journey continue to unfold and impact me. I deeply resent and find ludicrous that my perspective and views on child welfare are now considered 'radical' when, in the 1980s – the decade during which I undertook my social work studies at that very conventional tertiary institution, The University of Melbourne – the same perspective was commonplace.

Adoption is not child-focused. It is not the best option for meeting the needs of children who are unable to be raised safely in the care of their families, irrespective of what pro-adoption lobbyists and right-wing think-tanks would have us believe. For example, *Adoption Rethink* (2014) is a research review conducted by bioethicist Dr Greg Pike, commissioned by Women's Forum Australia – a self-declared 'independent' think-tank. *Adoption Rethink* takes a strongly pro-adoption stance in the context of a highly selective and superficial approach to its review of adoption research and literature, much of which is outdated and not relevant to the unique Australian context. *Adoption Rethink* is a substantial but flawed piece of work which lacks critical analysis. Yet, it is being actively promoted by Women's Forum Australia in the campaign seeking change to adoption legislation and policy across Australia.[41]

Meanwhile, Adopt Change is increasingly ramping up the celebrity endorsement and media components of its campaign. It boasts a stable of celebrity ambassadors, predominantly from the film and other media industries, both domestic and overseas. Many of these ambassadors are adoptive parents and

41 Press release (dated 07 November 2014) on Women's Forum Australia website <http://www.womensforumaustralia.org/media/AUSTRALIA%20NEEDS%20AN%20ADOPTION%20RETHINK.pdf>.

some are adoptees – all present as proud to push the positives of their own adoption experiences as if representative of all adoption journeys. There is a notable absence of 'relinquishing' parents among the supporters of Adopt Change. Still, it is easy to overlook this deficit with the distraction of recent big name product endorsements of its campaign. US brand Kiehl's is currently selling Limited Edition Ultra Facial Cream and, in collaboration with Sydney model, Bambi Northwood-Blyth, and her fashion designer husband, Dan Single, has produced a series of vintage-inspired Harley Davidson leather jackets to be showcased later this year on a joyride around Australia by the couple "with a gaggle of celebrities in tow" – with the net proceeds going to Adopt Change. The aim is to make adoption easier; the appeal is to everyone from beauties to bikers. Indeed, the mantra is:

> Every child deserves a permanent loving family … the goal is to push through ethical, open adoption and get the thousands of children currently in foster care into the legally binding embrace of the potential parents who are longing to adopt them.[42]

Never mind that the children in foster care were born into families who love them. Never mind that the most ethical goal is to seek and support the children's safe return to their families of origin. Never mind that adoption is always forced on the child, regardless of whether 'open' or 'closed'. Never mind that the very basis of adoption is unethical: the violation of children's universal rights, family connections and identities. Never mind that the underlying assumption of the pro-adoption campaign is that the families of children in foster care do not deserve to raise these children, while prospective adoptive families are entitled to do so.

With at least two public relations and/or advertising

42 Style Magazine (12 July 2015). Sourced from Press Reader <http://www.pressreader.com/australia/style-magazine/20150712/281556584491640/TextView>.

companies currently engaged by Adopt Change,[43] I expect the celebrity media hype promoting their particular brand of adoption awareness will have reached saturation point even before National Adoption Awareness Week – indeed, National Adoption Awareness Month – rolls around in November 2015. Still, I am reassured that I am not alone in my perspective on lobbyists. Geoffrey Watson, SC, who has a close understanding of the way in which the lobbyist industry works, has observed that lobbyist organisations often have only "a specious credibility." He reminds us that it is easy to become a lobbyist or lobbyist organisation, but cautions that "there's no ethical check. We make a mistake in thinking that lobbyists are an acceptable part of our democratic process." I share Watson's offence at the notion "that there is an implied freedom under our constitution that extends to allowing wealthy people to use their money to buy access" to government policy and decision makers.[44]

I acknowledge that it is not well known in the general community, but there is a very good long-term alternative care option for vulnerable children currently available in Victoria which has long been preferable to adoption: permanent care. Permanent Care Orders come under the jurisdiction of the Children's Court. They involve the transfer of custody and guardianship to the permanent caregivers. Custody involves the responsibility for day-to-day care and decision-making in relation to a child. Guardianship provides for the long-term welfare of the child and involves decisions relating to education, religious upbringing, etc. *In essence, permanent care is adoption without the bad bits – it provides stable and secure nurturing for the child, while preserving continuity of the child's identity and relationships with his or her family of origin, including their name at birth.* This is crucial to upholding the rights of the child

43 Sammway <http://www.sammway.com.au/>; and Special Group <http://www.specialgroup.com.au/>.

44 Geoffrey Watson is quoted in Mike Seccombe (2015).

as enshrined in the *UN Convention on the Rights of the Child*, and in ensuring the child's short- and long-term psychological well-being.

Governments have a dual responsibility to children. Firstly, they have a responsibility to facilitate adequate parenting of children within their own families. This includes the provision of appropriate and adequate supports to the family for a reasonable length of time in the event that they have a child identified through the state's child protection system as being at risk of neglect or abuse. Where it is subsequently deemed by the child protection authorities that it is not possible for the child to be raised safely and securely by their own parents or extended family, the state also has a responsibility to minimise further harm to the child and provide him or her with alternative family care which is suitably safe, secure and nurturing. However, the decision to remove a child from their parents and extended family network is a major one, irrespective of the level of abuse or neglect to which the child has been subject, or their age at the time of removal. It is well known in professional social work, psychology and psychiatric circles that the very act of separating a child from their family causes trauma to the child, which impacts neurological and psychological development.[45] Thus, where the state intervenes by removing a child from his or her family for the purpose of protecting that child, it has a fundamental responsibility to be primarily child-focussed in the alternative care that it subsequently provides to the child.

Adoption is fundamentally prospective parent-focussed. Even in the 20 or so cases of local adoption per year in Victoria that occur outside the child protection system (usually newborns/infants relinquished by young single women/unmarried couples), I maintain that adoption is not child-focussed.

45 A good introduction to trauma-informed practice in relation to children is available from the website of the Australian Childhood Trauma Group <http://www.theactgroup.com.au/>.

There is inherent contrariness in the situation whereby birth parents who volunteer to give up their child for adoption because they consider themselves lacking the capacity to raise that child (which they decided to carry to birth, rather than terminate early in their pregnancy) are, nevertheless, still considered by responsible authorities as having the capacity to make a decision which is in the best interests of their child. Yet, this decision is irrevocable and will impact the child for the duration of his or her entire life, even though in making this decision they – the parents – are abrogating their responsibilities to care for that child (though not their future opportunity to have other children that they may decide to raise themselves). It seems to me to be a case of 'all care and no responsibility'. Even in cases where the relinquishing parents have a significant intellectual or psychiatric impairment which would negatively impact their capacity to parent adequately, or the child has been genuinely abandoned and their parents/family are not known or able to be identified, adoption is often considered the best option by and/or for the birth parents and their extended family. However, the legal severing of the child's identity and connection with their birth family, even where unknown at the time of placement, cannot be considered to be in the long-term best interests of the child. What if the child successfully searches for and contacts their family of origin later in life? The fact of their adoption as an infant would preclude the opportunity for them to legally reclaim their true identity and heritage. From the child's perspective, I believe all such cases would be better dealt with via a Parenting Order under the *Family Law Act 1975*.

The principles of permanent care best meet the rights and interests of children deemed by competent child protection authorities unable to remain in the care of their parents or extended families. Best practice implementation of Permanent Care Orders – including maintaining a child-centred rather than service-centred focus, timeliness of decision-making, and ongoing support to all parties – requires further strengthening and above all, resourcing. Notwithstanding the process of developing the legislation without proper public consultation and the outrageous anomaly of adoption being listed third in the hierarchy of permanency objectives, a number of the amendments made under the Napthine government to the *Children, Youth and Families Act 2005* (to be implemented in March 2016) were designed with such strengthening in mind. The need for additional resourcing to properly implement these improvements was recognised in the first budget (in May 2015) of the Andrews government. This budget delivered a massive funding injection to children's and family services – to prevent children from entering out-of-home care as much as to provide better quality care for children who do so.

The permanent care framework already exists in Victoria and could be implemented in the other states and territories of Australia as well. This was, in fact, done in the Northern Territory earlier in 2015 – though apparently rather too hastily, given it has been reported that there was insufficient community consultation and the subsequent legislation "does not include safeguards to ensure that permanent care orders are only made as a last resort; and protect the connection to culture and family of Aboriginal children who end up in the permanent care of non-Aboriginal carers."[46] Clearly, further improvements to the NT legislation are required.

Regardless, there is no need for Australia to persevere with the unethical and unsustainable practice of adoption. In fact, there are strong arguments to abandon it altogether. Australia must do better for its vulnerable children; it must remain cognisant of Julia Gillard's profound words in her 2013 National Apology:

> We resolve, as a nation, to do all in our power to make sure these practices are never repeated. In facing future challenges, we will remember the lessons of family separation. Our focus will

46 See Hurley (2015).

be on protecting the fundamental rights of children and on the importance of the child's right to know and be cared for by his or her parents.

The significance of adoption in Australia should be confined to history. I look forward to the day when 'adoption' is a word no longer used in the present context of child and family welfare policies and practice but, rather, is relegated to discussions of Australia's dark past. Only then will we, as a modern Western society, be truly able to focus on how best to uphold the universal rights of vulnerable children in meeting their needs for long-term care.

The continuing practice of adoption in Australia – even in much lower numbers than prior to the 1980s – has allowed politicians and the general community to delude themselves that there are minimal, if any, negative impacts from separation for either the children or their families of origin. In turn, this has enabled governments to revert to practices which divest them of their duty to address the ongoing consequences of their own child protection practices by transferring all legal responsibilities for the children to adoptive parents. However, intrinsic to Victorian Permanent Care Orders is acceptance that all parties – the children, their families of origin and their permanent care families – will always be somewhat vulnerable and deserving of ongoing support, including that which facilitates the maintenance of positive relationships between them. In turn, this helps the children to overcome the trauma they inevitably experience in relation to being separated from their birth families and enhances the quality of their upbringings.

It is time for Australians to reject the practice of adoption and its inherently antiquated notions of entitlement to and ownership of children. It is time for Australia to sever this link with the insidious market in babies and children. Children are not commodities to be procured or chattels to be owned and re-labelled. Rather, children are the most vulnerable of all human beings and they deserve to be treated with the utmost care, respect and dignity. The general community may view adoption as a positive at best, or benign at worst, means for family formation. But this rationale is neither respectful nor accurate for the children concerned, nor for their families and communities of origin. Children are born with forever families – the parents who created them and their extended family members. No sleight of hand with the issuance of a new birth certificate can legitimately alter the facts of one's biological and genetic heritage, even if it can hide or obscure them. Similarly, the positives involved in adoption cannot cancel out the negatives also involved, even if they are presented in a way that deceives both the adoptive parents and the broader community.

Adoption has had its day in this country. In fact, adoption has had its century in this country, and I do mean the previous – twentieth – century. It is time, once and for all, to shift the focus of permanency planning for vulnerable children away from adoption and fully commit to permanent care. It is not good enough to settle for 'modernising' adoption legislation. It is time to embark upon a system-wide reform of the family and children's service system to embrace a truly child-focused approach. It is time to do away with the silo approach to program funding which matches children to available placements – which matches children to prospective families, rather than prospective families to children. It is time to transition to a 'one-door' approach to the recruitment, training, support and matching of caregiving families to the vulnerable children identified as requiring care outside their kinship networks.[47] It is time for the service-based support systems for families and children in Australia to undergo a revolution – a revolution in which adoption plays no part.

47 For more on the 'one-door' approach, see Shenker, McLeod and Hussey (2012); and Smith and Sturmfels (2010).

APPENDIX I

Prime Minister Julia Gillard's National Apology Speech including the National Apology for Forced Adoptions (21 March 2013)

I thank Shane Mortimer and Kelly Littlemore for the welcome to country and, in a spirit of reconciliation, acknowledge the traditional owners of this land on which we meet, and I acknowledge elders past and present.

The national significance of this occasion is reflected in the many people here today. I acknowledge this parliament's presiding officers: Anna Burke, Speaker of the House of Representatives; Senator the Hon. John Hogg, President of the Senate. Many members of the government are here today. They include Jenny Macklin, the Minister for Families, Community Services and Indigenous Affairs and Minister for Disability Reform; Mark Butler, the Minister for Mental Health, Minister for Housing and Homelessness and Minister for Social Inclusion; Mark Dreyfus QC, the Attorney-General; Nicola Roxon, our former Attorney-General; and many other ministers and government members.

I acknowledge the Leader of the Opposition and other members of the opposition present here today. I acknowledge also members of other parties and independent members, along with distinguished guests. Above all, let me acknowledge all of you–every Australian who has travelled here today, every Australian who is listening or watching at home–because you know the sorrow and suffering of forced adoption.

In just over an hour's time, the following words of apology will be moved in the Senate and the House of Representatives:

1. Today, this parliament, on behalf of the Australian people, takes responsibility and apologises for the policies and practices that forced the separation of mothers from their babies, which created a lifelong legacy of pain and suffering.
2. We acknowledge the profound effects of these policies and practices on fathers.
3. And we recognise the hurt these actions caused to brothers and sisters, grandparents, partners and extended family members.
4. We deplore the shameful practices that denied you, the mothers, your fundamental rights and responsibilities to love and care for your children. You were not legally or socially acknowledged as their mothers. And you were yourselves deprived of care and support.
5. To you, the mothers who were betrayed by a system that gave you no choice and subjected you to manipulation, mistreatment and malpractice, we apologise.
6. We say sorry to you, the mothers who were denied knowledge of your rights, which meant you could not provide informed consent. You were given false assurances. You were forced to endure the coercion and brutality of practices that were unethical, dishonest and in many cases illegal.
7. We know you have suffered enduring effects from these practices forced upon you by others. For the loss, the grief, the disempowerment, the stigmatisation and the guilt, we say sorry.
8. To each of you who were adopted or removed, who were led to believe your mother had rejected you and who were denied the opportunity to grow up with your family and community of origin and to connect with your culture, we say sorry.
9. We apologise to the sons and daughters who grew up not knowing how much you were wanted and loved.

10. We acknowledge that many of you still experience a constant struggle with identity, uncertainty and loss, and feel a persistent tension between loyalty to one family and yearning for another.
11. To you, the fathers, who were excluded from the lives of your children and deprived of the dignity of recognition on your children's birth records, we say sorry. We acknowledge your loss and grief.
12. We recognise that the consequences of forced adoption practices continue to resonate through many, many lives. To you, the siblings, grandparents, partners and other family members who have shared in the pain and suffering of your loved ones or who were unable to share their lives, we say sorry.
13. Many are still grieving. Some families will be lost to one another forever. To those of you who face the difficulties of reconnecting with family and establishing on-going relationships, we say sorry.
14. We offer this apology in the hope that it will assist your healing and in order to shine a light on a dark period of our nation's history.
15. To those who have fought for the truth to be heard, we hear you now. We acknowledge that many of you have suffered in silence for far too long.
16. We are saddened that many others are no longer here to share this moment. In particular, we remember those affected by these practices who took their own lives. Our profound sympathies go to their families.
17. To redress the shameful mistakes of the past, we are committed to ensuring that all those affected get the help they need, including access to specialist counselling services and support, the ability to find the truth in freely available records and assistance in reconnecting with lost family.
18. We resolve, as a nation, to do all in our power to make

sure these practices are never repeated. In facing future challenges, we will remember the lessons of family separation. Our focus will be on protecting the fundamental rights of children and on the importance of the child's right to know and be cared for by his or her parents.

19. With profound sadness and remorse, we offer you all our unreserved apology.

Friends, this Apology is extended in good faith and deep humility. It will be a profound act of moral insight by a nation searching its conscience. It will stand in the name of all Australians as a sign of our willingness to right an old wrong and face a hard truth.

As Australians, we are used to celebrating past glories and triumphs, and so we should. We are a great nation. But we must also be a good nation. Therefore, we must face the negative features of our past without hesitation or reserve. That is why the period since 2008 has been so distinctive–because it has been a moment of healing and accountability in the life of our nation.

For a country, just as for a person, it takes a lot of courage to say we are sorry. We do not like to admit we were mistaken or misguided. Yet this is part of the process of a nation growing up: holding the mirror to ourselves and our past, and not flinching from what we see. Friends, what we see in that mirror is deeply shameful and distressing: a story of suffering and unbearable loss–but ultimately a story of strength, as those affected by forced adoptions found their voice, organised and shared their experiences and, by speaking truth to power, brought about the Apology we offer today.

This story had its beginnings in a wrongful belief that women could be separated from their babies and it would all be for the best. Instead, these churches and charities, families, medical staff and bureaucrats struck at the most primal and sacred bond there is: the bond between a mother and her baby. Those affected by forced adoption came from all walks of life: from the city or the country, people who were born here or migrated here and people who were Indigenous Australians, from different faiths and social classes. For the most part, the women who lost their babies were young–very young indeed. They were often pregnant and sometimes even drugged. They faced so many voices telling them to surrender, even though their own lonely voice shouted from the depths of their being to hold on to the new life they had created.

Too often they did not see their baby's face. They could not sooth their baby's first cries, never felt their baby's warmth or smelt their baby's skin. They could not give their own baby a name. These babies grew up with other names and in other homes, creating a sense of abandonment and loss that sometimes could never be made whole.

Friends, today we will hear the motion moved in parliament and many other words spoken by those of us who lead. But today we also listen to the words and stories of those who have waited so long to be heard, like the members of the Reference Group personally affected by forced adoption, who I met earlier today. Lizzy Brew, Katherine Rendell and Christine Cole told me how their children were wrenched away so soon after birth, how they were denied basic support and advice, how the removal of their children led to a lifetime of anguish and pain.

Their experiences echo the stories told in the Senate report, stories that speak to us with startling power and moral force–like Linda Bryant, who testified of the devastating moment her baby was taken away. She said: 'When I had my child she was removed. All I saw was the top of her head; I knew she had black hair.' So often, that brief glimpse was the final time those mothers would ever see their children. In institutions around Australia, women were made to perform menial labour in kitchens and laundries until their baby arrived. As Margaret

Bishop said: 'It felt like a kind of penance. In recent years, I have occasionally passed what was then the Medindi Maternity Hospital, and it generates a deep sadness in me and an odd feeling that it was a Dickensian tale about somebody else.' Margaret McGrath described being confined within the Holy Cross home, where life was, to use her words, 'harsh, punitive and impersonal'. Yet this was sunny postwar Australia, where we were going to the beach and driving our new Holdens and listening to Johnny O'Keefe.

Friends, as the time for birth came, these babies would be snatched away before they had even held them in their arms. Sometimes consent was achieved by forgery or fraud. Sometimes women signed adoption papers whilst under the influence of medication. Most common of all was the bullying arrogance of a society that presumed to know what was best. Margaret Nonas was told she was selfish. Linda Ngata was told she was too young and would be a bad mother. Some mothers returned home to be ostracised and to be judged. And, despite all the coercion, many mothers were haunted by guilt for having 'given away' their child–guilt because, in the words of Louise Greenup, they did not 'buck the system or fight'.

Friends, the hurt did not simply last for a few days or weeks. This was a wound that would not heal. Kim Lawrence told the Senate Committee: 'The pain never goes away, that we all gave away our babies. We were told to forget what had happened, but we cannot. It will be with us all our lives.' Carolyn Brown never forgot her son: She said: 'I was always looking and wondering if he was alive or dead. From then on every time I saw a baby, a little boy and even a grownup in the street, I would look to see if I could recognise him.' For decades, young mothers grew old haunted by loss, silently grieving in our suburbs and towns. And somewhere, perhaps even close by, their children grew up denied the bond that was their birth right. Instead, they lived with self-doubt and an uncertain identity, the feeling, as one child of forced adoption put it, 'that part of me is missing'. Some suffered sexual abuse at the hands of their adoptive parents or in state institutions. Many more endured the cruelty that only children can inflict on their peers: the words, 'Your mum's not your real mum; your real mum didn't want you; your parents aren't your real parents; they don't love you'–taunts vividly remembered decades later.

For so many children of forced adoption, the scars remain in adult life. Phil Evans described his life as a: rollercoaster ride of emotional trauma, indescribable fear, uncertainty, anxiety and self-sabotage in so many ways. Many others identified the paralysing effect of self-doubt and a fear of abandonment: 'It has held me back, stopped me growing and ensured that I have lived a life frozen.' I heard similar stories of disconnection and loss from Leigh Hubbard and Paul Howes today, the challenges of reconnecting with family, the struggles with self-identity and self-esteem, the difficulties with accessing records, challenges that even the highest levels of professional success have not been able to assuage or heal.

Friends, neither should we forget the fathers, brothers and sisters, grandparents and other relatives who were also affected as the impact of forced adoption cascaded through each family. Gary Coles, a father, told me today of the lack of acknowledgment that many fathers have experienced–how often fathers were ignored at the time of the birth, how their names were not included on birth certificates, how the veil of shame and forgetting was cast over their lives too.

My fellow Australians, no collection of words alone can undo all this damage or make whole the lives and families fractured by forced adoption or give back childhoods that were robbed of joy and laughter or make amends for the birthdays and Christmases and Mother's or Father's Days that have only brought a fresh wave of grief and loss. But by saying sorry we can correct the historical record. We can declare that these mothers did nothing wrong, that you loved your children and you always will.

And to the children of forced adoption, we can say that you deserved so much better. You deserved the chance to know, and love, your mother and father. We can promise you all that no generation of Australians will suffer the same pain and trauma that you did–the cruel, immoral practice of forced adoption that will have no place in this land anymore.

We also pledge resources to match today's words with actions. We will provide $5 million to improve access to specialist support and records-tracing for those affected by forced adoptions. And we will work with the states and territories to improve these services. The government will also deliver $5 million so that mental health professionals can better assist in caring for those affected by forced adoption. We will also provide $1.5 million for the National Archives to record the experiences of those affected by forced adoption through a special exhibition. That way, this chapter in our nation's history will never again be marginalised or forgotten again.

Friends, today's historic moment has only been made possible by the bravery of those who came forward to make the submissions to the Senate committee and the bravery too of those who could not come forward but who nurtured hope silently in their hearts. Because of your courage, Australia now knows the truth. The report prepared so brilliantly by Senator Siewert and the Senate committee records that truth for all to see.

This was further reinforced by the national consultations that Professor Nahum Mushin and his reference group undertook to draft the national Apology. Their guidance and advice to government on the drafting of the Apology have been invaluable. Any Australian who reads the Senate report or listens to your stories, as I have today, will be appalled by what was done to you. They will be shocked by your suffering. They will be saddened by your loss. But, most of all, they will marvel at your determination to fight for the respect of history.

They will draw strength from your example. And they will be inspired by the generous spirit in which you receive this Apology–because saying sorry is only ever complete when those who are wronged accept it. Through your courage and your grace, the time of neglect is over, and the work of healing can begin.

APPENDIX II

Opposition Leader Tony Abbott's Speech (21 March 2013)

Prime Minister, Shane Mortimer, parliamentary colleagues but, most of all, people impacted by the policies of forced adoption: your presence here today in such numbers and with such obvious power is a sign of how much this issue matters.

I add my own words to the eloquent and heartfelt statement that we have just heard from the Prime Minister. In 1977, someone very important to me had a baby that was adopted. A few years later, still unmarried, she had another baby that she raised herself because, having surrendered one child, she could not possibly do it again. The late Kathy Donnelly was a beautiful person and a fine mother who loved all her children. She deserved nothing but love and support, not coercive expectations, social stigma and–I say this with more than a pang of personal guilt–men in her life who had failed to live up to their responsibilities.

I have not known a more courageous or a more admirable person ever. Her predicament and that of Daniel, the son she did not know for 27 years, was so frequent in an era when abortion was difficult and contraception unavailable and when, for all sorts of reasons, marriage was thought to be impossible. We are all living with that legacy.

I cannot imagine a grief greater than that of a parent and a child parted from each other. I cannot imagine an ache greater than the fear that 'mum didn't want me', especially, since it was not true. But hundreds of thousands of Australians have been adopted, often because their mothers had no real choice or were denied any choice, and that means that there are hundreds of thousands of mothers who hardly knew their children and hundreds of thousands of children who hardly knew their mothers.

This is a tragedy for them and for our nation, and we must atone for it. It was never simply 'for the best'. The people who claimed that it was should have known better. Some of them did know better, but they persisted, despite the avoidable pain that was inflicted on hundreds of thousands of people. There is no stronger bond than that between mother and child and, at least while children are young, there is no more important relationship. There are no first- and second-class mothers. There are no first- or second-class children. Every child deserves a mother's love, and every mother has the right to raise her child. We know it now, and we should have known it then. It should never have been presumed–presumed–that some mothers were incapable of raising their child, because, as everyone here knows only too well, there was presumption and there was coercion, by families, by charities, by peers and by the conditions that governments placed upon people.

The harder something is–and few things are harder than raising a child alone–the more people should have had our support, not our judgement. We were hard-hearted and we were judgemental, and that is why we should apologise. We did inflict pain on those we loved and on those we had a responsibility for. For some, we turned what should been the wonderful experience of new life into something filled with shame. Instead of love, there was reproach; instead of support, rejection; instead of celebration, silence; and instead of justice, wrongdoing.

So today, our nation acknowledges that this was wrong and that we are sorry. Today, we accept responsibility for the pain, the suffering and the grief reverberating through tens of thousands of Australian families. On behalf of the nation, I join the Prime Minister in apologising.

We also honour everyone who through the years has demonstrated an unyielding determination not to be crushed by this injustice and to bring our failures to light. Today, your courage has prevailed. We honour the birth parents, including fathers, who have always loved their children. We honour those adoptive parents who have tried to do the right thing by their children. And we honour all the children who have tried. I honour the parents who have always loved their children.

Member/s of the audience interjecting–

Mr Abbott: The last thing I would wish to do is to cause pain to people who have suffered too much pain already and I am happy to retract it.

We honour the parents, including the fathers, who have always loved their children. We honour those adoptive parents who have tried to do the right thing by their children. And we honour all the children who have tried in their own ways to find their own place in a complex and confusing world.

There are big lessons here, now and for the future. I have just learnt some myself a moment ago. We should not think that it is only previous generations that have made mistakes. Part of apologising for old mistakes is striving to avoid new ones. And I will strive, madam, to avoid new ones.

Whenever adoptions take place, they have to be chosen and they have to be for the right reasons. People have a right to make choices and they deserve our love and respect whatever choices they make.

Ladies and gentlemen, my friends, we cannot avoid making judgements. They should be much more honest ones in the future than they have been in the past. That way, we will not be perfect but we should be better. Ladies and gentlemen, it is an honour to be involved in today's Apology. I sincerely hope that it can bring self-respect where there was shame, peace where there was anger and reassurance where there was reproach. May it be a part of the healing process for our nation and for all of us.

GLOSSARY

AASW	Australian Association of Social Workers
AIS	The Victorian Adoption Information Service (now known as FIND)
ARMS	Australian Relinquishing Mothers Society
ASIO	Australian Security Intelligence Organisation
BDM	The Victorian Department of Births Deaths and Marriages
CEO	Chief Executive Officer
COAG	Council of Australian Governments
CSMC	Council of the Single Mother and Her Child
CSV	The Victorian Department of Community Services Victoria (now known as DHHS)
DHHS	The Victorian Department of Health and Human Services
DHS	The Victorian Department of Human Services (now known as DHHS)
FIND	Family Information Networks and Discovery
FOI	Freedom of Information
Hague Convention	Hague Convention on Protection of Children and Co-operation in Respect of Intercountry Adoption
ICAS	The Victorian Intercountry Adoption Service
IVF	In vitro fertilisation
LGBTI	Lesbian Gay Bisexual Transsexual Intersex
MP	Member of Parliament
NAAW	National Adoption Awareness Week
NSW	New South Wales
NT	Northern Territory
QVH	Queen Victoria Hospital

SC	Senior Counsel
UN	United Nations
UNICEF	United Nations Children's Fund (formerly known as the United Nations International Children's Emergency Fund)
US	United States (of America)
USA	United States of America
VANISH	Victorian Adoption Network for Information and Self Help (formerly known as V.A.N.I.S.H.)

BIBLIOGRAPHY

Abbott, Tony (21 March 2013) Speech, Sourced from Attorney-General's Department, Australian Government <http://www.ag.gov.au/About/ForcedAdoptionsApology/Pages/default.aspx>.

Abbott, Tony (25 January 2015) 'Intercountry Adoption Support Service to Help Families' Press Release <http://www.pm.gov.au/media/2015-01-25/intercountry-adoption-support-service-help-families>.

Adopt Change <http://www.adoptchange.org.au/OurHistoryVisionMission>.

Adoption Act 1984 (Victoria) <http://www5.austlii.edu.au/au/legis/vic/consol_act/aa1984107/>.

Adoption Amendment Act 2013 (Victoria) <http://www.google.com.au/rl?sa=t&rct=j&q=&esrc=s&source=web&cd=1&ved=0CB4QFjAAahUKEwi60ff_pMPHAhVGFJQKHY3YAZ8&url=http%3A%2F%2Fwww.legislation.vic.gov.au%2Fdomino%2Fweb_notes%2Fldms%2Fpubstatbook.nsf%2Ff932b66241ecf1b7ca256e92000e23be%2F00b546911d857c68ca257b6c0021d7bb%2F%24file%2F13-025a.docx&ei=m-DbVfqXI8ao0ASNsYf4CQ&usg=AFQjCNFg3W7zGHvsYia1JVa2HN7AEn2LEA>.

Allan, Sonia (5 August 2014) 'Commercial surrogacy is not the way forward' *The Age*, Melbourne <http://newsstore.fairfax.com.au/apps/viewDocument.ac;jsessionid=D530CDAB1DFC9173EC6F8A9306D43BD9?sy=afr&pb=all_ffx&dt=selectRange&dr=1month&so=relevance&sf=text&sf=headline&rc=10&rm=200&sp=brs&cls=165&clsPage=1&docID=AGE140805RA7LP3BA2KC>.

Attorney-General's Department, Australian Government <https://www.ag.gov.au/FamiliesAndMarriage/IntercountryAdoption/Pages/reforms.aspx>.

Australian Bureau of Statistics <http://www.abs.gov.au/ausstats/abs@.nsf/Lookup/by%20Subject/1301.0~2012~Main%20Features~Population%20size%20and%20growth~47//>.

Australian Childhood Trauma Group <http://www.theactgroup.com.au/>.

Australian Citizenship Amendment (Intercountry Adoption) Act 2015 <https://www.comlaw.gov.au/Details/C2015A00007>.

Australian Institute of Health and Welfare (2013) 'Adoptions Australia 2012-13' Child Welfare Series No. 57, Australian Government, Canberra <http://www.aihw.gov.au/WorkArea/DownloadAsset.aspx?id=60129545513>.

Centre for Excellence in Child and Family Welfare (14 August 2014) *Fact Sheet* <http://www.cfecfw.asn.au/sites/default/files/Fact%20Sheet%20-%20CYF%20(Permanent%20Care%20and%20Other%20Measures).pdf>.

Children, Youth and Families Act 2005 <http://www.austlii.edu.au/au/legis/vic/consol_act/cyafa2005252/>.

Cossins, Annie (2013) *The Baby Farmers: A chilling tale of missing babies, shameful secrets and murder in 19th century Australia*, Allen & Unwin, Sydney.

Cummins, Philip, Dorothy Scott OAM and Mr Bill Scales AO (January 2012) *Report of the Protecting Victoria's Vulnerable Children Inquiry Report: Volumes 1–3* <http://www.childprotectioninquiry.vic.gov.au/report-pvvc-inquiry.html>.

Department of Human Services (circa late 1990s) *Adoption and Permanent Care Fact Sheets*, Victorian Government.

Department of Human Services (circa 2012) *Adoption and Permanent Care Learning Guide, Part 3*, Victorian Government <http://www.dhs.vic.gov.au/__data/assets/pdf_file/0007/582064/3-Permanent-Care-APC-Learning-Guide.pdf>.

Department of the Prime Minister and Cabinet (April 2014) *Report of the Interdepartmental Committee on Intercountry Adoption*, Australian Government <https://www.dpmc.gov.au/sites/default/files/publications/idc_report_intercountry_adoption.pdf>.

Department of Reproductive Health and Research (2013) *Global and regional estimates of violence against women: prevalence and health effects of intimate partner violence and non-partner sexual violence*, World Health Organization, Italy <http://apps.who.int/iris/bitstream/10665/85239/1/9789241564625_eng.pdf>.

Department of Social Services, Australian Government <https://www.dss.gov.au/our-responsibilities/families-and-children/programmes-services/parenting/intercountry-adoption>.

Fitsell, Ann (1994) 'Sexual attraction following reunion (GSA)' Excerpt from *Proceedings of the Fifth Australian Adoption Conference*, Sydney <http://jigsawqld.server101.com/Jigsawqld/NL10.html>.

Foreign Correspondent (21 April 2015) ABC <http://www.abc.net.au/foreign/content/2015/s4220901.htm>.

Fronek, Patricia and Denise Cuthbert (2013) 'Apologies for Forced Adoption Practices: Implications for Contemporary Intercountry Adoption' *Australian Social Work*, 66 (3), pp. 402–414 <http://www.australiansadopt.org/documents/ApologiesforForcedAdoptionPracticesImplicationsforcontemporaryintercountryadoptionsvvs2.pdf>.

Fronek, Patricia, Denise Cuthbert and Mary Keyes (8 September 2014) 'Australia puts children at risk by 'freeing up' the adoption market' *The Conversation (Australia)* <http://theconversation.com/australia-puts-children-at-risk-by-freeing-up-the-adoption-market-31064>.

Geary, Belinda Grant (23 May 2015) 'End of the road for cycling champion Cadel Evans and his wife: Long distance career blamed for ending 10-year marriage... but they vow to stay friends for adopted son' <http://www.dailymail.co.uk/news/article-3093678/End-road-cycling-

champion-Cadel-wife-Long-distance-career-spells-end-couple-s-ten-year-marriage-vow-stay-friends-adopted-son.html#ixzz3ehLjjuNA>.

Gillard, Julia (21 March 2013) 'National Apology for Forced Adoptions' Speech, Sourced from Attorney-General's Department, Australian Government <http://www.ag.gov.au/About/ForcedAdoptionsApology/Pages/default.aspx>.

Graham, Thomas (2014) 'Where darkness resides: suicide and being adopted – is there a connection of elevated risk?' *Australian Journal of Adoption*, 8 (2), pp. 1–24 <http://www.nla.gov.au/openpublish/index.php/aja/article/viewFile/3520/4131>.

Hague Convention on Protection of Children and Co-operation in Respect of Intercountry Adoption (1993) <http://www.hcch.net/index_en.php?act=conventions.text&cid=69>.

Han, Esther (10 November 2012) 'Foreign adoptees want apology for forced separation' *Sunday Age*, Melbourne.

Higgins, Daryl (March 2010, amended 30 April 2010) *Impact of Past Adoption Practices: Summary of key issues from Australian research: Final report, A report to the Australian Government Department of Families, Housing, Community Services and Indigenous Affairs*, Australian Institute of Family Studies. <https://www.dss.gov.au/our-responsibilities/families-and-children/publications-articles/impact-of-past-adoption-practices-summary-of-key-issues-from-australian-research>.

Higgins, Daryl (2011) 'Unfit mothers … unjust practices? Key issues from Australian research on the impact of past adoption practices' Australian Institute of Family Studies, *Family Matters*, No. 87 <https://aifs.gov.au/publications/family-matters/issue-87/unfit-mothers-unjust-practices>.

House of Representatives Standing Committee on Family and Human Services (November 2005) *Overseas Adoption in Australia: Report on the inquiry into adoption of children from overseas*, The Parliament of the Commonwealth of Australia, Canberra, Australia <http://www.aph.gov.au/parliamentary_business/committees/house_of_representatives_committees?url=fhs/./adoption/prelims.htm>.

Hurley, Monique (24 April 2015) 'The Problem with Permanent Care Orders in the Northern Territory' *Right Now: Human Rights in Australia* <http://rightnow.org.au/topics/children-and-youth/the-problem-with-permanent-care-orders-in-the-northern-territory-2/>.

Huynh, Pascal. Teaser for documentary film 'As If Born To' <https://vimeo.com/120993591>.

Huynh, Pascal. Online panel discussions:
Panel 1: Questioning the Sustainability of the Concept of Adoption <https://www.youtube.com/watch?v=nSKgUrUWHGk>,
Panel 2: Being an Australian pre-1980s Local Adoptee <https://www.youtube.com/watch?v=8qoq6mVPeVw>,
Panel 3: About the Reality of Intercountry Adoptees <https://www.youtube.com/watch?v=_BK9doze4Nc>,
Panel 4: The Issues with Intercountry Adoption <https://www.youtube.com/watch?v=VPGrD4GRxFA>.

Inglis, Kate (1984) *Living mistakes: Mothers who consented to adoption*, North Sydney, NSW, Allen and Unwin.

Intercountry Adoption Australia <http://www.intercountryadoption.gov.au/>.

Jackman, Deborra-Lee (2011) 'Australia's poor adoption record' First published by ABC Online *The Drum* Unleashed (14 January 2008) <http://www.abc.net.au/news/2008-01-14/36942>, Re-published in Justin Healey (ed) *Adoption Issues: Issues in Society*, Vol. 326, The Spinney Press, NSW, pp. 42–43.

Kenny, Pauline, Daryl Higgins, Carol Soloff and Reem Sweid (August 2012) *Past adoption experiences: National Research Study on the Service Response to Past Adoption Practices, Research Report* No. 21, Australian Institute of Family Studies, Australian Government, Melbourne <https://aifs.gov.au/publications/past-adoption-experiences>.

Klein, Renate (20 August 2014) 'Wombs are not merely suitcases for babies' *The Age* <http://newsstore.fairfax.com.au/apps/viewDocument.ac;jsessionid=46800F9C706FDDB86A811242601D0489?sy=afr&pb=all_ffx&dt=selectRange&dr=1month&so=relevance&sf=text&sf=headline&rc=10&rm=200&sp=brs&cls=5049&clsPage=1&docID=AGE140820S06EO5GUM9I>.

Leicester, Dawn and Penny Mackieson (2013) *Real Women Love Footy*, Lothian Books, Melbourne.

Mackieson, Penny (11 August, 2014a) 'The overseas adoption option' *Overland Journal* <https://overland.org.au/2014/08/the-overseas-adoption-option/>.

Mackieson, Penny (Summer, 2014b) 'Surrogacy and adoption' *AASW National Bulletin*, 24 (4), pp. 15–16.

Milligan, Louise (04 June 2015) 'Adoption needs overhaul or abandoning say people adopted as children' ABC *7.30* <http://www.abc.net.au/7.30/content/2015/s4249194.htm>.

Needham, Kirsty (29 March 2014) 'Radical new laws to raise adoption rate dramatically' *The Sydney Morning Herald* <http://www.smh.com.au/comment/radical-new-laws-to-raise-adoption-rate-dramatically-20140327-zqnnx.html>.

Pearson, Allison (10 August 2014) 'Give Gammy the fairytale ending he deserves' *Sunday Age*.

Phillips, Janet and Penny Vandenbroek (14 October 2014) 'Domestic, family and sexual violence in Australia: an overview of the issues' Research Paper Series 2014–15, Department of Parliamentary Services, Parliament of Australia <http://parlinfo.aph.gov.au/parlInfo/download/library/prspub/3447585/upload_binary/3447585.pdf;fileType=application/pdf>.

Pike, Gregory K (2014) *Adoption Rethink*, Women's Forum Australia <http://www.womensforumaustralia.com/adoption>.

Quartly, Marian, Shurlee Swain and Denise Cuthbert (2013) *The Market in Babies: Stories of Australian Adoption*, Monash University Publishing, Melbourne, Australia.

Sammway <http://www.sammway.com.au/>.

Seccombe, Mike (04 July 2015) 'Barton Deakin, the Coalition's "evil twin" lobby firm' *The Saturday Paper* <https://www.thesaturdaypaper.com.au/news/politics/2015/07/04/barton-deakin-the-coalitions-evil-twin-lobby-firm/14359320002084?utm_source=The+Saturday+Briefing&utm_campaign=0597f81395-The_Saturday_Briefing_04_07_2015&utm_medium=email&utm_term=0_6de0204698-0597f81395-303243913#.VZc8C4sViM9>.

Shenker, Sheri, Kathryn McLeod and Carmel Hussey (2012) 'One Door and a Continuum of Care: A New Model of Out of Home Care for Children' *Australian Journal of Adoption*, 6 (1) <http://www.nla.gov.au/openpublish/index.php/aja/article/viewFile/2554/3000>.

Smith, Susan and Debbie Sturmfels (2010) 'One Door: A unified approach for caregivers' *Children Australia*, 35 (2), pp. 43–47.

Special Group <http://www.specialgroup.com.au/>.

State Library of Victoria <http://guides.slv.vic.gov.au/content.php?pid=55757&sid=408113>.

Style Magazine (12 July 2015) Sourced from Press Reader <http://www.pressreader.com/australia/style-magazine/20150712/281556584491640/TextView>.

Swain, Shurlee (2012) 'Snapshots from the Long History of Adoption in Australia' *Australian Journal of* Adoption, 6 (1) <http://www.nla.gov.au/openpublish/index.php/aja/article/viewArticle/2550>.

Swan, Jonathan (19 December 2013) 'PM Tony Abbott pledges to ease the way for overseas adoption after campaign by actor Deborra-Lee Furness and husband Hugh Jackman' *The Sydney Morning Herald* <http://www.smh.com.au/federal-politics/political-news/pm-tony-abbott-pledges-to-ease-the-way-for-overseas-adoption-after-campaign-by-actor-deborralee-furness-and-husband-hugh-jackman-20131219-2zmlw.html>.

Szego, Julie (14 August 2014) 'Scary, yes, but a womb for rent makes sense' *The Age* <http://www.theage.com.au/comment/it-sounds-scary-but-renting-a-womb-makes-sense-20140812-1036ai.html>.

The Age (12 August 2014) 'A baby factory or a legitimate service?' Editorial <http://www.theage.com.au/comment/the-age-editorial/a-baby-factory-or-a-legitimate-service-20140811-3disj.html>.

The Drum (22 March 2013) ABC <http://www.abc.net.au/news/2013-03-22/gillard-adoption-apology/4587876>.

The Saturday Briefing (04 July 2015) *The Saturday Paper* email.

The Senate Community Affairs References Committee (February 2012) *Commonwealth Contribution to Former Forced Adoption Policies and Practices*, Australian Government <http://www.aph.gov.au/Parliamentary_Business/Committees/Senate/Community_Affairs/Completed_inquiries/2010-13/commcontribformerforcedadoption/report/index>.

The Wheeler Centre (12 November 2013) 'Forming Families: National Adoption Awareness Week' <http://wheelercentre.com/videos/video/the-fifth-estate-forming-families-national-adoption-awareness-week/>.

United Nations Convention on the Rights of the Child (1989) <http://www.ohchr.org/en/professionalinterest/pages/crc.aspx>.

VANISH <http://vanish.org.au/about-vanish/history-of-vanish>.

Victorian Equal Opportunity and Human Rights Commission <http://www.humanrightscommission.vic.gov.au/index.php/human-rights>.

Women's Forum Australia (07 November 2014) Press release <http://www.womensforumaustralia.org/media/AUSTRALIA%20NEEDS%20AN%20ADOPTION%20RETHINK.pdf>.

Wroe, David and Tony Wright (22 March 2013) 'Forced adoption apology was PM at her finest' *The Age* <http://www.smh.com.au/federal-politics/political-news/forced-adoptions-apology-was-pm-at-her-finest-20130321-2giu5.html>.

INDEX

Women as Wombs: Reproductive Technology and the Battle over Women's Freedom

Janice Raymond

Under the guise of liberatory science, the biomedical establishment is using women's bodies as the biological laboratories of the future.

Women as Wombs is a scathing analysis of high-tech biomedical reproductive techniques. It provides groundbreaking insights into the debate over reproductive technology and its ethical, legal, and political implications.

Raymond asserts that far from being liberatory issues of 'choice', these techniques – including in vitro fertilization, surrogacy, trafficking in children and sex selection – are a threat to women's basic human rights.

A strongly written, carefully reasoned critique of the reproductive liberalism that … lies behind current concepts of reproductive choice.

— K. Kaufmann, *San Francisco Chronicle Review*

A passionate yet coolly reasoned polemic, Janice G Raymond's Women as Wombs *offers an array of alarming insights regarding the worldwide implications of new reproductive technologies.*

— Emily Jeremiah, *Journal of the Association for Research on Mothering*

…it is hard to resist her conclusion that many reproductive experiments can represent another form of violence against women. Highly recommended.

— *Library Review Journal*

Rights: World
ISBN: 9781875559411
eBook: available

Angels of Power
and other reproductive creations

Susan Hawthorne and Renate Klein (eds)

In the tradition of Mary Shelley's *Frankenstein*, the contributors to the book rework images of the body. Imagination, vision and a sense of the absurd come together and demonstrate that women can resist the power of god-like scientists and carry us into a different future: one in which human diversity is valued; and one in which women's bodies are not used for experimentation simply because we are here.

In *Angels of Power*, feminist authors from Australia, Canada and the USA write fiction, drama and poetry around the issue of new reproductive technologies.

Angels of Power *should head the reading list of any course in ethics and reproductive technology.*

– Karen Lines, *Editions*

If collections such as this can render the ethical issues imaginatively through fiction they will have contributed significantly to this important debate, as this one does.

– Irina Dunn, Journalist

Rights: World
ISBN: 9781875559008
eBook: available

Being and Being Bought:
Prostitution, Surrogacy and the Split Self

Kajsa Ekis Ekman

Grounded in the reality of the violence and abuse inherent in prostitution–and reeling from the death of a friend to prostitution in Spain–Kajsa Ekis Ekman exposes the many lies in the 'sex work' scenario. Trade unions aren't trade unions. Groups for prostituted women are simultaneously groups for brothel owners. And prostitution is always presented from a woman's point of view. The men who buy sex are left out.

Ekis Ekman argues that the Self must be split from the body to make it possible to sell your body without selling yourself. The body becomes sex. Sex becomes a service. The story of the sex worker says: the Split Self is not only possible, it is the ideal.

Turning to the practice of surrogate motherhood, Kajsa Ekis Ekman identifies the same components: that the woman is neither connected to her own body nor to the child she grows in her body and gives birth to. Surrogacy becomes an extended form of prostitution. In this capitalist creation story, the parent is the one who pays. The product sold is not sex but a baby. Ekis Ekman asks: why should this not be called child trafficking?

Being and Being Bought *gives an incisive portrayal, not only of the sex and surrogacy industries, but also of the arguments used to justify them both, arguments that Kajsa Ekis Ekman skilfully and comprehensively pulverises. Her work is overflowing with humanity and empathy for some of the most downtrodden women and girls in the world.*

– Laura Fitzgerald, *Irish Socialist Party*

Rights: World English Language
ISBN: 9781742198767
eBook: available

Kick the Tin

Doris Kartinyeri

When Doris Kartinyeri was a month old, her mother died. The family gathered to mourn their loss and welcome the new baby home. But Doris never arrived to live with her family – she was stolen from the hospital and placed in Colebrook Home, where she stayed for the next fourteen years.

The legacy of being a member of the Stolen Generations continued for Doris as she was placed in white homes as a virtual slave, struggled through relationships and suffered with anxiety and mental illness.

'Kick the tin' was a game Doris Kartinyeri played in the Colebrook Home. This is a life that has been kicked around. It is the compelling and sometimes witty memoir of an Aboriginal woman's courageous journey, a journey into the soul of an individual to find meaning and substance after the loss of everything the rest of us take for granted.

Kick the Tin *is a story of courage and survival, powerfully demonstrating how the human spirit can soar despite all the injuries and injustices which threaten to drag it down.*

– Lowitja O'Donoghue

Kick the Tin *is a quiet, powerful book.*

– Charlotte Simpson, *Belletrista.com*

Rights: World
ISBN: 9781875559954
eBook: available

Glory

Sarah Brill

She lies in the bed and she is sick. Sicker than she's ever been. But with the sickness comes a pain and in that pain she finds a glory. And it's the glory that gets her through.

When her body heals and she is out of hospital and home with her family, she needs to seek out a new glory, a stronger glory. She finds it in starvation.

A story of one girl's struggle with herself, her life as an adopted child, and her family. And the story of a family's struggle with a daughter/sister they can never hope to fully understand.

Youthful suicide, anorexia and drug abuse are dangerous topics for the novelist to handle ... Playwright Sarah Brill boldly and successfully tackles all three in this first novel ... A writer to watch.

– Lucy Sussex, *The Age*

Sarah speaks from the inside of a muddled teenager's head. And which teenager is not muddled? Every parent, however confident must read this book – it will open up their minds and help them understand their children. If you think you know your kid – this book will expose the reality – you really don't.

– Reader Review, *Amazon*

Rights: World
ISBN: 9781876756253
eBook: available

If you would like to know more about Spinifex Press write for a free catalogue or visit our website.

SPINIFEX PRESS
PO Box 212 North Melbourne
Victoria 3051 Australia
www.spinifexpress.com.au